STOCK MARKET REBOUND

MOMENTUM STOCK INVESTING WITH COVERED CALLS

SCOTT DOUGLAS

DISCLAIMER

As stipulated by law, I cannot and do not make any guarantees about your ability to get results or earn any money from the ideas, information, tools or strategies presented.

The risk of loss in trading securities and options can be substantial. Please consider all relevant risk factors, including your own personal financial situation, before investing or trading. Stocks and options do involve risk and are not suitable for all investors.

Use caution and always consult your accountant, lawyer or professional advisor before acting on this or any information related to a lifestyle change or your finances.

CONTENTS

INTRODUCTION

What's the best investment you could make? It's not stocks, real estate or precious metals. The answer may surprise you.

What matters the most is your financial education. If you're wanting to improve your current financial situation, reduce your debt load and better provide for your family, then Stock Market Rebound may provide you with a number of the answers.

The coronavirus pandemic of 2020 and collapse of the global economy has left many devastated. If this makes your teeth grind like a pepper mill, you're not alone. Most Americans lost fortunes. Many have no clue as to how they're going to get back to even.

This guide takes you by the hand and walks you step-by-step through an investment approach that takes advantage of any major stock market correction, not just our current crash. During these uncertain times, one thing is certain for sure. The stock market always bounces back.

And one of the best ways to capitalize on any market rebound is through momentum stock investing. You're about to discover how to capture upside price swings in fast-growing market leaders that are the best of breed in their respective industries.

Not only that, I'll also be sharing insights into how to use a couple of conservative option strategies to generate an additional stream of monthly income into your brokerage account. I've always been a big advocate for layering positions - using one investment strategy along with an interrelated one.

Selling covered calls on stock you own allows you to layer on an income generation strategy with growth in stock price appreciation. Why not tap into the best of two worlds so you can accelerate your recovery or wealth creation even faster?

There's no better time to invest in the stock market than right after a major meltdown. Stock values are often unfairly depressed. Opportunity knocks. But how do you take advantage of what Mr. Market has dealt everyone?

Trying to figure out how to rebuild what has been lost can be as difficult as swimming upstream in Jell-O. Fortunately, you need not do so on your own. That's where the sage advice and insights in this resource come in handy. No longer do you or your family have to struggle needlessly.

In this guide, you're about to discover:

- What specific industries show the most promise post-pandemic.
- What types of businesses and industries to avoid in 2020.
- How to identify and invest in fast-growing market leaders.
- What simple criteria you need to use for safely entering and exiting positions.
- How to select an appropriate covered call strategy that'll optimize any position.
- What it takes to develop an effective investment plan for momentum plays.

I know you want to be as cautious as a tightrope walker with a severe itch. This is why any investment approach worth its weight in gold needs to take one crucial item into consideration. Preservation of your hard-earned capital must be foremost on your mind.

This means knowing when you need to cut any losses,

how to minimize transaction fees and using specific exit strategies to capture gains.

The interesting aspect of covered calls is they're not only a conservative means of generating monthly income, but they also offer you downside protection for your holdings. You'll find out how to build an element of safety into each of your positions. Knowing how to better preserve your capital should give you a greater sense of peace of mind.

My stock investment journey has exposed me to a myriad of investment educators and gurus, dating back to the 90's. Back then the options market was in its infancy for the do-it-yourself investor like yourself. Fast forward to today and the current economic climate has lowered most investment barriers. No longer do you need to spend over $100 per option transaction.

In fact, most online discount brokers are offering transaction fees as low as pennies on the dollar. This factor alone makes it more advantageous now more than ever to learn how to sell option contracts on stock you control. It's almost like being that enviable landlord who rents out apartments for monthly income.

The momentum investing approach described in your guide is not new. Momentum stock investing has been around for decades. What is new is the context in which the strategy is being used. The world has changed. It's no longer business as usual. Industries will come and go. Society is adapting to a new normal.

Knowing how to apply any momentum investment approach to this changing landscape becomes the challenge. Stock Market Rebound looks at how to effectively use momentum plays to improve your overall financial situation in this new social and economic context. This is why the first few chapters of your book focus on how life is evolving after this unprecedented pandemic and which industries will benefit moving forward. These are the prospects to explore. Fast-growing, young businesses capable of adapting to a new world economy are the ones you'll learn how to identify.

After exploring what industries and what not to select as potential investments, the next step is to be zeroing in on specific stock picks. The key to stock selection is keeping the process as simple as possible yet producing a high probability of success. Much of the focus of your guide is on using just a handful of selection criteria.

You'll be exposed to both fundamental and technical indicators. These commonly used indicators will narrow down your options to a few choice prospects with a high likelihood of producing substantial returns.

As you have probably already experienced, the stock market has not moved upward in a straight line since its inception. It moves upward but with periodic swings like the waves of the ocean rising and falling.

Right now, we're experiencing one of those troughs. There's no denying, things have been rough for the markets in the first half of 2020. However, I'm as excited as a seagull with a French fry at the prospect of what 2021 will bring. Every major stock market correction creates incredible portfolio growth opportunities.

This is especially so for the do-it-yourself momentum investor armed with an arsenal of momentum and call option strategies designed to quickly rebuild losses or accelerate portfolio growth. And your guide looks at how you can optimize your returns by using a combination of momentum and option plays.

Once you've completed this guide to investing in momentum stocks and learned how to maintain momentum growth through covered call options, you'll be in the enviable position of taking back control of your financial affairs. Who could say no to creating a better life for you and your loved ones with a little financial education?

Do you realize how much opportunity is waiting for you right now? Unfortunately, if you don't tap into this information now, you may regret missing out. The stock market is sure to rally. Time to take advantage of a stock market rebound.

So, let me ask you, are you ready for a change? Are you ready to discover how you can generate significant returns using some simple strategies? Don't just lie around like an Egyptian mummy in a sarcophagus. Let's get started today exploring the wonderful world of stock investing. Opportunity awaits.

1

CREATING YOUR OWN ECONOMIC STIMULUS PACKAGE

MANY OF US feel powerless when faced with economic hardship. Tumbling stock markets threatening to wipe out months, if not years, of market gains can take its toll on our psyche. Turmoil in the financial markets often leaves us wondering what we can do to bounce back.

There is a solution. In order to benefit from a quick rebound, you must take a proactive approach to getting back to even. You must take the initiative to create your own economic stimulus package. One that'll take advantage of over-reaction, panic and fear occurring in the stock market. Time to profit from the downturn.

Markets will turn around and bounce back. The question is: Do you want to be a part of the rebound? If so, you'll need to set yourself up for success in preparation for the re-surgency in the economy. Momentum stock investing coupled with the income-producing potential of selling covered calls on under-valued stock you own is one potential solution.

But before you can effectively dive deep into the momentum stock investment process, it'll help to provide an overview of the entire process. Some basic background knowledge into the three fundamental investment approaches and how trend or momentum investing fits into the overall investment scheme gives you some context. Otherwise, you have no more chance than a one-legged, one-armed player in a football game.

Gaining greater perspective of how the overall economic situation could play out is vital to the investment process, for which ever approach you decide to embrace. Without having a real sense of what is unfolding in the economy and the markets, you're limited as to effective options to pursue. What follows is that clarity and those insights.

As well, once you have a better idea as to what momentum or trend investing has to offer, you can better explore how to profit from the recent economic downturn AND also benefit from future market shakeups that typically occur every five to seven years. Let's begin by briefly outlining why a momentum investing approach works.

How can you profit from the recent economic downturn?

Your guide describes step-by-step how to use a momentum stock investing approach in combination with covered call writing. With momentum investing you'll be looking at investing in fast growing companies when they're undervalued and at attractive prices. You'll be attempting to catch the wave to recovery and beyond with stocks shown to have strong revenue growth potential. When this happens, the value of your holding increases as stock price climbs.

The second aspect of this overall investment approach is to use the monthly income generation potential of selling covered calls on stock you own. Doing so, helps to accelerate your gains in the market. We'll be focusing our efforts on using only two conservative call option strategies to create an additional attractive income stream from your holdings.

Fundamental to the whole investment process is being able to follow an investment system, which emphasizes adhering to five basic criteria, namely being:

1. Simple to implement.
2. Easy to automate.
3. Effective in producing consistent results.
4. Quick to learn.
5. Offering protection of capital.

What you're about to explore is a resource geared towards the average American's ability to invest in the markets, especially after a downturn in the markets.

Time to explore how momentum investing fits into the three well-known approaches to investing in the stock market.

How can we categorize stock investment approaches?

Stock investment approaches can be assigned to three general categories of value, income and growth investing. Each provides the budding investor - that's you - with different opportunities offering:

- Different risk - reward profiles.
- Varying investment holding periods.
- And the use of various stock investment strategies within each approach.

What follows is a simplified explanation of these three

common approaches and how momentum investing fits in. It's an important consideration.

Value Investing:

The main objective of value investing is to purchase shares of undervalued businesses below fair market price and hold them long-term until the shares can be sold above their true intrinsic value at a profit.

The top five key factors of value investing are:

- A primary focus on capital preservation, which is achieved by buying equities with a large margin of safety below their fair market value. A margin of safety refers to a current stock price that is more than 25% less than the stock's estimated intrinsic value or retail price.
- Investors select businesses with solid fundamentals in the areas of book value, debt levels, and return on capital invested over a minimum 5-year period.
- A value investor is looking at long-term holding periods for the stock, typically 5 to 10 years.
- The type of investor favored is one with a low risk tolerance and who is also patient and disciplined. Finding good value stocks

requires you commit to putting in extensive research time.

- Value investors profit best from the stock price cycling from being undervalued to overvalued.

In a nutshell, value investing often takes a lot of time for identifying favourable equities to invest in. It also typically requires years to realize significant profits.

It can be as slow as a huge blob of molasses on a two-degree slope. Not quite what we're looking for as an investment approach.

Income Investing:

The primary objective of income investing is to generate a regular, income stream from typically mature companies that consistently pay a small portion of profits back to the shareholders in the form of dividends.

The key factors of income investing are:

- A main focus on regular income production. This is often seen with quarterly dividend payouts. An emphasis on capital preservation by investing in companies that have a long solid track record is of primary concern.
- Income investors select mature businesses with consistent earnings, sales and cash flow

over long periods of 10 to 20 years and these companies have a historical record of paying good dividends.

- The stock holding period is usually long-term, typically greater than 10 years.
- The type of investor favoured is one with a low risk tolerance, who is typically looking for consistent income generation.
- Income investors profit best from mature businesses not greatly affected by economic cycles and who have a solid track record of consistently paying out dividends.

Growth Investing:

The primary objective of growth investing is to purchase shares in companies experiencing higher than market average earnings growth due to a major change affecting the industry. Growth investors seek out businesses in their infancy of their growth phase, giving them the greatest potential to grow and become more stable mature companies down the road.

The top five factors of growth investing are:

- A main focus on capital appreciation through increased share price. This is often seen in companies experiencing a major positive change in their industry, which typically happens as a result of new market trends, expanding international markets, or new technological breakthroughs.

- Growth investors like to select specialized businesses or industries experiencing positive change, They typically experience superior growth in earnings, sales with a strong possibility of high growth of any invested capital.
- The stock holding period is often medium-term, typically lasting 2 to 5 years.
- The type of investor favoured is one with a moderate risk tolerance who's looking for capital appreciation through stock price appreciation.
- Growth investors profit best from younger companies seeing the benefits from a major market change enabling them to grow earnings and invested capital above the market average.

Each approach has a place in an investor's portfolio, giving the majority of stock investors the opportunity to make money in the stock market depending on one's level of expertise, involvement and patience.

Some approaches do take longer to see the fruits of

one's labor. The question begging to be asked is: How does momentum or trend investing fit in?

What is momentum investing all about?

In a nutshell, momentum investing is based on a growth approach that takes advantage of downward market corrections to ride stock prices up in fast-growing companies. The overall strategy you're about to discover also entails using an income investing approach incorporating option strategies to generate higher returns than just a growth approach. It's an important consideration.

Ideally, you're looking for growing companies rebounding from a major stock market correction, which are market leaders in their industry. Market leaders have the general market and stock price momentum behind them. Big institutional buyers look for stocks within a specific sector or industry the overall market has fallen in love with. These stocks are in favour with Mr. Market and are showing positive growth trends in world demand for their products or services being offered.

Take 2011 and 2012 for example, which saw the mobile internet growing worldwide. This resulted in many technology stocks like Apple moving higher as a result of being in favour with the overall market players. Who wouldn't want to get in at the ground level with this stock? You'd be as excited as a puppy at a picnic with the growth the company experienced over the past decade.

The same can be said of drug and pharmaceutical companies benefitting from the COVID-19 pandemic. Several companies have been caught up in developing lucrative vaccines or providing testing supplies to overwhelmed healthcare institutions and businesses.

Market leaders tend to be companies who are benefiting the most from worldwide demand of the sale of their products and services. They also tend to be the best businesses within their industry or what many analysts call "best of breed" businesses. These businesses not only have the momentum of Mr. Market working in their favour, but they also have certain factors in place, which ensure a certain level of ongoing productivity and stock price appreciation.

We can loosely group these factors into three categories, namely:

1. Solid business financials or fundamentals. Key growth ratios like Return on Invested Capital, Book Value per Share, Revenue, and Earnings per Share are showing consistent double-digit growth rates, as well as long-term debt levels being under control.

2. A solid, shareholder-oriented management team that values its employees' contributions. The best CEO's have their shareholder's interest at heart and not their ego or the bonuses they might receive.

3. A sustainable competitive advantage. Best of breed businesses in a particular industry have a significant competitive advantage. This can be easily verified by looking at the growth rates for earnings, sales, and cash flow.

Market leaders have the staying power to be profitable over time, which in turn increases your profitability potential as an investor. Before we delve into what types of businesses make good trend investing candidates, let's touch on some of the pros and cons of momentum investing. Sound like a plan, Sam I am.

What are the pros and cons of a momentum investing approach?

The two key advantages of trend investing are:

- This approach is generally easier to set up and monitor than many other investment systems. It can save you time and some frustration down the road in reducing the amount of time required to do your due diligence and monitor your positions.

- Your actual returns can be easily measured since the holding period for momentum stocks is often less than one year.

As a side note, the term "actual returns" refers to the dollar amount you have generated from the purchase and sale of equities and/or the sale of option contracts on stock you own. These actual dollar amounts have been deposited into your brokerage account.

On the flip side are "paper returns". These are the theoretical returns your brokerage account is displaying based on the current value of each position you're holding. Paper returns do not become realized or actual returns until you exit your position and the proceeds from the transaction are deposited into your brokerage account as cash.

This is an important distinction to make. Despite experiencing paper losses during a stock market meltdown, you have not lost any hard-earned cash until you take action to exit your position and the proceeds from the transaction now become an actual financial loss.

Some of the disadvantages of using a momentum trading approach are:

1. It's often associated with higher turnover rates

for holding onto specific equities. This can translate into higher overall transaction fees, which can potentially put a dent in your overall returns. This is why paying attention to transaction fees is so important for increasing your bottom line.

2. When stock market volatility increases after a major market correction, it's more challenging to use the momentum strategy. This book's approach places an emphasis on capital preservation by minimizing losses through pre-set stop limits. So, monitoring these safeguards is necessary. You want to feel as safe as a nun in a room full of eunuchs.

3. Should you have a very conservative risk profile, using a momentum trading approach can be a difficult strategy to use from a psychological point of view. If you're a passive, "buy and forget about it" investor, momentum trading may not be your cup of tea.

As a quick side note, you'll learn more about stop losses in upcoming chapters. A stop loss is simply a sell order for a holding like a stock when the stock price drops down to a pre-set limit. This strategy limits your losses as a stock drops in price.

Momentum trading opens up the possibility of

generating significant returns from your holdings in a short period of time. The best momentum trading approaches not only capitalize on stock price appreciation, but also have safeguards in place to ensure capital loss is kept to a minimum.

You're about to find out just how to do that. But before we look at how to safely trade on momentum, let's briefly touch on what businesses make good candidates for this particular approach.

What should you be looking for in a potential momentum stock pick?

Businesses ideally suited for momentum growth plays all tend to be young companies who are rapidly growing their sales and fall into one of three categories:

1. **Emerging industries.** New technology companies offer some of the best growth opportunities for investors. Consumers at the retail level may be jumping at the opportunity to acquire the latest, greatest, new fang-dangled gizmo to hit the market. Non tech businesses are also embracing new technologies to improve their bottom line, offer new products and services, or create new efficiencies.

2. **Formula companies.** Those businesses operating at a regional level with a successful, replicable formula that can be scaled nationally do well with a momentum investing approach. Look for small to mid-size market cap regional companies who are expanding nationally or globally.

3. **Rapid reversal companies.** Those businesses initially hit with substantial losses of market share due to a temporary global setback can rebound quickly once a level of stability and confidence returns to the market. Unfairly beaten up companies can rally quickly to pre-crash levels when dragged down by overall market sentiment.

The term "market cap" refers to the value of a business based on how much capitalization the company has. Capitalization is calculated by multiplying the total number of outstanding shares issued by the company by the current share price in the stock market.

Small cap companies have market caps under $2 billion. They make good candidates for aggressive growth plays as most institutional investors tend to shy away from these rapid risers until they have a proven track record.

Mid cap companies fall into the $1 billion to $5 billion

market cap range. And large cap businesses have market caps in excess of $10 billion. These businesses have a history of dependable earnings, solid reputations, and strong long-term financials. Of note is that the parameters provided are fluid and not fixed. They depend on the overall state of affairs in the stock market and as such should be used as guidelines.

Which brings us to the question:

What stocks are typically not good candidates?

Those businesses that are well-established in the national and international arena typically do not make the ideal candidates for momentum plays. Often, these mature companies have already experienced their peak rapid growth years. Because of this, they tend to attract or entice investors to stay invested by offering quarterly dividends.

Dividends are a means by which investors can benefit from a regular stream of income being deposited into their brokerage account, usually on a quarterly basis. This cash deposit can then be used to pay for one's lifestyle or re-invested into other equity plays.

Although dividend-paying stocks can provide an attractive income stream, there are better options available to investors looking to capitalize on rebounds in the market. You'll discover how you can profit from rapidly rising stocks that also trade in the options market to generate an attractive income stream along with capital appreciation. A momentum approach provides a higher probability of capital appreciation in the short-term.

But before we look at the specific steps you can follow, it makes sense to first identify how the current economic crisis is providing opportunities and where to look for specific momentum plays. Ready for a dose of insights?

2

UNDERSTANDING THE STATE OF AFFAIRS

ONCE YOU HAVE a deep understanding as to how certain industries are affected by a downturn in the economy, you'll be in a better position to make well-informed decisions about investment prospects. What follows is a discussion as to what the global economy has recently experienced with the COVID-19 outbreak and how it will affect your decision-making in the context of general momentum investment possibilities.

Whether the catalyst for a major market correction is a pandemic, housing crisis or financial institution meltdown, the principles of analysis remain the same. This is why this resource will serve you well for years to come. Knowing how to address future stock market corrections is paramount to your success as an investor. You don't want to be as surprised and shocked as a sardine that went to sleep in the ocean only to awaken in a delicatessen.

Your take-away from this discussion should be to look at how each downturn in the markets affects economic sectors differently. Armed with some fundamental insights, you'll be in a better position to identify those industries having a higher probability of a faster rebound than others.

Knowing which stocks are likely to rebound faster in any down market, means that you can use a momentum trading approach to invest more effectively. You're creating your edge in the markets.

Greater confidence in the choices you make equates to greater peace of mind in uncertain times. So, let me ask you right now, are you one of those individuals who would love to increase your chances of success?

Let's see how you can tap into major corrections of the business or economic cycle to make money in the markets.

What is the business/ economic cycle?

The business or economic cycle refers to the rise and fall in output production of goods and services in the economy. Business cycles are generally measured using directional changes to the gross domestic product (GDP), either nominal or adjusted for inflation. The business cycle is characterized by periods of expansion and contraction. During expansion periods, the economy experiences growth, while periods of contraction indicate economic decline or what has become known as a recession.

The economic cycle can be described as being composed of five or six stages following a specific order as follows:

1. **Expansion:** Expansion occurs when there is an increase in employment opportunities, income gains, overall production, and sales. The economy has a steady flow or access to money supply and stock investment is booming. When the economy is growing, people generally pay their debts on time.

During the expansion phase, the gross domestic product (GDP), which measures economic output, is increasing. The GDP growth rate is in a healthy 2 to 3 percent range. Unemployment reaches its natural rate of 3.5 to 4.5 percent. Inflation remains near its 2 percent target level. The stock market is in a "bull market", whereby stock prices are increasing over time in each of the eleven economic sectors.

Since the 1990s, the average expansion in the U.S. has lasted 95 months (or over 7 years). This is encouraging news for stock investors as the periods of expansion since 1945 have risen from an average of 58 months to almost double. It gets me as excited as a muskrat family at the local mud slide.

2. Peak: When the economy has reached the maximum level of growth or there are external global factors that bear down on the economy, growth stalls. Many refer to it as the month when the expansion transitions into the contraction phase. Often stock market prices hit their highest level, but economic indicators stop growing. This causes concern in big business with many starting to restructure as the economy's growth starts to reverse.

When the economy overheats with a GDP growth rate in excess of 3 percent, many stock investors are in a state of "irrational exuberance." Inflation may rise to greater than 2 percent and has been known to reach double digit values. When the economy heats up under these conditions, asset bubbles may be created. Investors end up pumping money into over-inflated investments often driven by greed as opposed to sound financial fundamentals. It's time for a market correction.

3. Recession: A recession is a period of economic and business contraction. During a recession, unemployment rises, production slows down, sales decrease because of a decline in demand, and incomes become stagnant and may even decline. The average period of contraction has lasted 11 months in recent recessionary periods. Recessions often offer stock investors opportunities to purchase equities at a discount. When using a momentum approach to investing, significant stock price appreciation becomes easier to attain. Would this situation increase your chances of success? You bet your sweet bippy it would.

4. Depression: A depression doesn't always follow a recession. If it does, economic growth continues to drop while unemployment rises and production plummets. Both consumers and businesses find it challenging to secure credit. With decreasing sales and trade, bankruptcies start to increase. Mass layoffs make headline news. As a result, consumer confidence and investment levels also drop.

As economic growth weakens, the GDP growth falls below 2 percent. At the point when it turns negative, is what many economists call a recession. With rising unemployment rates, businesses wait to hire new workers until they're sure the recession or depression is over. Stocks enter a bear market as investors sell their positions placing their remaining capital in fixed assets like bonds and treasury bills.

5. Trough: The trough period marks the end of the recession/depression. Economists consider it to be the month when the economy transitions from the contraction phase to the expansion phase. It indicates when the economy hits bottom. The slowing ceases in the trough. The next stage of expansion begins to gradually emerge. It can feel as slow as trying to cross the Sahara on a pogo stick.

6. Recovery: The final stage of the economic cycle sees the economy starts to turn around. Low commodity, wholesale and retail prices spur an increase in demand. Employment begins to return to normal levels. Production levels start to rise, and lenders start to provide capital to fuel an expanding economy. The recovery stage marks the end of one business cycle leading into the expansion phase once again. Stock markets may see a transition from showing neutral signs of growth to entering a bull phase. Remember, bulls are good, bears are bad.

The National Bureau of Economic Research (NBER) determines the dates for business cycles in the United States. Committee members take into account real GDP, income, employment, industrial production, and wholesale-retail sales, along with debt and market measures to help understand the causes of expansions and ensuing contractions.

It takes time to analyze all this information, so the NBER doesn't tell you the phase until after it has started. You can look at the indicators yourself to determine what phase of the business cycle we are currently in. Just keep in mind that it's a lagging indicator which confirms what has occurred in the last economic quarter.

The NBER identifies a recession as:

> "a significant decline in economic activity spread across the economy, lasting more than a few months, normally visible in real GDP, real income, employment, industrial production."

When this period of time is extended outward beyond a few months, the economy often enters a period of depression.

Now that you have an idea as to how the economic cycle affects the state of the economy and business growth, it's time to look at how the stock market typically reacts to overcoming a recessionary period of time and bounces back. The rebound is what gets me excited bouncing from foot to foot like a child in need of a potty.

When will the economy be good again?

We're treading on new ground when it comes to how the global economy will recover from the COVID-19 pandemic. The question being asked in the spring of 2020 was: Is the stock market going to experience a gradual or rapid recovery? Will we see a re-surgency in the markets as quickly as the crash that occurred in March of 2020?

According to Barry Sternlicht, the former CEO of the investment fund Starwood Capital Group, he envisioned a V-shaped bounce back for the market. Many who support the notion of a rapid market recovery are as he puts it: "using this as buying opportunities in the public market."

He argued that both low interest rates and oil prices are conducive to seeing businesses turn around quickly.

Unfortunately, most economists and business leaders do not share his optimism. Too much damage to the infrastructure of the economy was done. This is both bad and good news for you.

The bad news is having to deal with the aftermath of a global shutdown with economic hardship affecting most Americans. The good news is in being able to take advantage of incredible growth opportunities in the stock market as the economy and markets rebound. A more re-assuring feeling.

Former top economist to President Barack Obama, Jason Furman, believes the current recovery will likely have three stages:

A contraction phase: This is what Americans experienced in the spring of 2020. Millions of Americans lost their jobs, lives were put on hold, and both business and consumer spending fell to unprecedented levels. The stock market dropped precipitously within a short period of time creating incredible buy opportunities for certain stocks unfairly beaten up in the ensuing panic.

A partial bounce back: The summer of 2020 is seeing a re-opening of the economy. Once again, hiring, spending and investing are re-igniting the recovery. This is the ideal time for stock market investors to position themselves in fast-growing equities during this period of re-surgency. Unfortunately, the bounce back is unlikely to bring the economy all the way back to where it was in January 2020. Don't expect it to move at hypersonic speed.

A long slog: After a relatively rapid initial improvement, the stock market will in all probability take a long time to return to pre-coronavirus levels. Unemployment, wages, consumer confidence and discretional spending will require time to work through. Simply put, the more employees laid off, the more households running out of savings, the more people falling behind on their bills, the longer the slog of recovery.

If history is any indicator, expect a recovery period of at least 11 months, which is the average period of time a recession has historically lasted since 1945. In all likelihood, a complete recovery probably won't occur until we have inoculated a significant portion of the population against the virus with an effective vaccine. Any such vaccine could take twelve to eighteen months to develop and distribute worldwide.

The timeline for the partial rebound and long slog is difficult to know. The partial recovery is likely to look robust at first, with parts of the economy being able to snap back to levels approximating their pre-crisis state.

While it's not possible to rule out a rapid and complete return to normalcy with a V-shaped recovery, most experts consider it unlikely. Too much structural damage has been done to the economy as a whole with certain jobs and businesses being lost, never to come back again. Many Americans will be worse off than they were before or even afraid to resume their lives as they once lived them.

Although the picture looks bleak in the eyes of the average consumer, any meltdown in the stock market presents incredible investment opportunities. When you know what to look for and how to capitalize on those potentially lucrative investments, you set yourself up for significant gains. Remaining ignorant is like the frog who thinks its puddle to be a great sea. Time to allow your mind to change. Don't allow it to fossilize like lava.

What's being done to deal with the pandemic?

The first order of business in dealing with the global pandemic was to apply social distancing measures in all communities in the spring of 2020. This practice allowed for the over-whelmed healthcare systems to more effectively deal with the onslaught of coronavirus patients entering hospitals.

We heard constant mention of being vigilant in flattening the curve. We were encouraged to do our part in minimizing infection rates by staying at home and away from others. These social distancing guidelines, while being tough to swallow, were a necessary step in minimizing the impact on healthcare providers.

With social distancing measures in place, governments across the world scrambled to ramp up healthcare capacity. Despite the economic crash caused by the pandemic, some businesses actually bolstered their bottom lines by being in industries of high demand. Those businesses having the capacity to produce personal protection equipment, virus test kits, and ventilators, to name a few, benefitted immensely from increased demand and production.

Not all industries were decimated by a meltdown in the stock market. This is great news for you. When you can analyze how economic sectors are being affected differently during a bear market, you position yourself to take advantage of mispricing's. I don't know about you, but this gets me more excited than being pampered with six square meals a day on a cruise ship.

As local jurisdictions began to get a handle on the number of COVID-19 cases coming across hospital thresholds by the fall of 2020, the second order of business was to provide widespread testing. By building testing capacity, communities were able to better detect and trace possible infections. Coupled with widespread testing for the virus was the rise of antibody testing for immunity.

Before the economy can resume anything approaching normalcy, the coronavirus outbreak will need to be firmly under control. When this breakthrough happens, consumer confidence in participating in the economy won't get them or their loved ones sick, will be bolstered. At this point and not before will you see a return to society's typical economic activity.

What are the 11 economic sectors?

Businesses in the stock market are loosely grouped with other like businesses into eleven economic sectors. These sectors are made up of businesses grouped in specific industries sharing common characteristics in the products and services being offered. Here's a quick rundown of each major sector and examples of fast-growing companies from the spring of 2020:

Materials:

Businesses belonging to this sector are those taking some sort of raw material or natural resource through a process to be used by other businesses or consumers. Companies dealing with mining, chemicals, logging, metals, and some oil & gas businesses fall into this category.

Examples of fast growers: Newmont Corp. (NEM) + International Flavors & Fragrances (IFF) + Sherwin-Williams Co. (SHW)

Industrials:

Businesses in the industrial sector fall into two categories, those who provide transportation services and infrastructure and those producing capital goods such as electrical equipment, industrial machinery or aircraft.

Examples of fast growers: Alaska Air Group Inc. (ALK) + Rockwell Automation Inc. (ROK) + Roper Technologies Inc. (ROP)

Healthcare:

This sector is made up of two broad aspects of health care. The first group of industries are the medical device manufacturers along with medical service providers. The second group of industries are the biotech and pharmaceutical companies that produce the drugs. Healthcare is made up of providers of equipment, drugs, insurance and medical facilities.

Examples of fast growers: Gilead Sciences Inc. (GILD) + Dentsply Sirona Inc. (XRAY) + Edwards Lifesciences Corp. (EW)

Consumer Discretionary:

Those businesses marketing their products and services to consumers, not businesses, fall into this category. What they sell is generally bought with discretionary income as opposed to being necessity purchases. Industries within this sector include automobiles, apparel, hotels, restaurants, leisure-related businesses and luxury goods.

Examples of fast growers: Harley Davidson Inc. (HOG) + Hasbro Inc. (HAS) + Expedia Group Inc. (EXPE)

Financials:

The financial sector is made up of businesses providing financial services to commercial and retail customers. The sector is made up of banks, investment companies, insurance providers and real estate firms.

Examples of fast growers: Assurant Inc. (AIZ) + Progressive Corp. (PGR) + Chubb Ltd. (CB)

Energy:

Companies in the energy sector produce or supply energy. The sector comprises businesses that provide services and equipment for the exploration, production, refining and marketing of primarily fossil fuels like coal, oil and natural gas.

Examples of fast growers: Helmerich & Payne Inc. (HP) + Kinder Morgan Inc. (KMI) + Valero Energy Corp. (VLO)

Information Technology:

Information technology businesses produce software, hardware or semiconductor equipment used by the Internet. Software support, computer design and data processing services are also a part of this information driven sector.

Examples of fast growers: ServiceNow Inc. (NOW) + NortonLifeLock Inc. (NLOK) + Cadence Design Systems Inc. (CDNS)

. . .

Communication Services:

Formerly known as the telecom sector, this sector is comprised of companies providing communication services through fixed-line, wireless, high bandwidth or fiber optic cable networks. It also includes media and entertainment companies.

Examples of fast growers: Fox Corp. (FOXA) + Netflix Inc. (NFLX) + Verizon Communications Inc. (VZ)

Real Estate:

Businesses involved in the purchase and sale of properties used for residential, commercial or industrial purposes fall into this category. The sector also includes those businesses who are involved in developing, appraising, marketing, leasing and managing properties.

Examples of fast growers: Apartment Investment & Management Co. (AIV) + Digital Realty Trust (DLR) + Federal Realty Investment Trust (FRT)

Consumer Staples:

Known as the defensive sector for its ability to better weather stock market recessions, it's made up of those companies producing food, beverage, and non-durable household or personal products. These products provide the necessities of life people required no matter whether the economy is doing poorly or well. This sector traditionally trails the overall stock market in the expansion phase of the economic cycle making them a questionable choice for momentum plays.

Examples of fast growers: Newell Brands Inc. (NWL) + Coca-Cola Inc. (KO) + Molson Coors Beverage Co. (TAP)

Utilities:

Businesses in this sector provide necessary services like water, electricity, natural gas and sewage to local communities. These capital-intensive businesses often have natural monopolies protecting them from outside competition. As such, they are highly regulated by local governments in their profit earning potential.

Examples of fast growers: Exelon Corp. (EXC) + Pinnacle West Capital Corp. (PNW) + NextEra Energy Inc. (NEE)

Institutional Investors and the Business Cycle.

Many institutional stock investors use the business cycle to profit from the market by choosing the right stocks at the right time.

For example, an institutional investor may choose to invest in certain commodities or technology stocks during the recovery phase because they may be cheap.

They may then decide to sell their positions once they've experienced a period of price appreciation in the stock market during the expansion phase.

When the economy is overheating and has reached its peak, many institutional investors using a long-term buy and hold approach, place their money into utilities, consumer staples, and healthcare. These specific sectors have historically outperformed the market during recessions. Businesses catering to consumers who rely on certain products and services to be available in good times and bad, benefit from recessionary periods because demand doesn't decrease even during times of instability.

That's all hunky dory for the big boys, but what about you - the upcoming retail investor? How should you approach investing so you can benefit from a downturn in the economy? Let's look at those industries hardest hit by this recent downturn in the stock market, along with those industries suffering the most, before we explore potential winners.

3

INDUSTRIES IMPACTED THE MOST

WHEN YOU HAVE A BETTER understanding as to how the economy has been impacted by recent developments in the global economy, you're in a more powerful position to invest in the stock market. Whether you're analyzing this recession or the next one, starting with an understanding of what has evolved and the impact on the markets is essential.

What follows is a basic analysis of what impact the novel coronavirus and ensuing collapse of the world economy has had on market investments.

The hardest hit companies - The BEACH stocks.

Some industries have been hit hard by recent developments in the stock market. It's as if these industries have been sidelined and gone on vacation.

Their sales collapsed like a punctured blister. A group of these industries, which at first appearance seem to be the hardest hit by the pandemic, have been aptly named the "beach stocks".

Those companies in the travel and entertainment industries have been hit the hardest during the novel coronavirus pandemic as a result of travel restrictions and social distancing. We can group these industries under the acronym BEACH, which stands for:

- Booking
- Entertainment & Live Events
- Airlines
- Cruises & Casinos
- Hotels & Resorts

With fewer tourists, limited travel and uncertainty around restrictions, these industries have seen massive drops in share price. For example, the holding company for Booking.com, OpenTable, Kayak and Priceline saw a sharp decline of over 35 percent in share price during the market meltdown in the spring of 2020.

Cancellations and postponements in the entertainment industry due to declining ticket sales for concerts, movies and other events all but shut down the industry on 2020. Even the multi-billion global movie industry suffered major losses in not being able to continue production. Revenue from Disney and Universal theme parks dried up completely once states imposed stay-at-home orders or restrictions to help contain the COVID-19 virus. A quick rebound is about as likely as a mouse falling in love with a cat.

Coincidentally, the price of crude oil plummeted during the pandemic as OPEC oil producers and Russia glutted the international market with cheap crude over a bitter pricing and production battle. The domestic oil industry is struggling to remain profitable in the wake of this price war.

One may think that both the airline and cruise industries, which rely heavily on the oil industry, would be jumping for joy at the price of a barrel of crude. Travel is closely linked to the oil industry, as transportation accounts for 60 percent of world demand.

Unfortunately, airlines and cruise lines have been negatively impacted by the travel restrictions being imposed worldwide. Both air travel and cruises dried up in the first half of 2020. Trying to make these industries competitive is like teaching an elephant to tap dance on a bar stool while juggling peanuts.

Coupled with these impacted industries are the hotels

and resorts, which saw reservations disappear in the wake of the pandemic due to strict travel restrictions.

The question many analysts are asking is: Will BEACH industries bounce back quickly as social distancing restrictions are eased or will businesses in these heavily affected industries experience a slow and painful recovery?

The travel and hospitality industries could experience a longer recession while other industries recover faster. It all depends on how quick people are to trust the safety of extensive travel for either pleasure or business. The sooner people feel confident about testing and infection tracing, the sooner these industries will be back to normal.

The same goes for restaurants, bars and coffee shops. It might be awhile before people are comfortable crowding into such establishments. Right now, it seems unlikely we'll see a rapid recovery of the BEACH industries. They seem to be as helpless as a lion without teeth.

Which Industries have changed radically moving forward?

We are seeing radical changes evolving in certain industries affected by the novel coronavirus pandemic. Four in particular offer the smart investor good prospects moving forward out of the pandemic crisis and they are:

- Education.
- Entertainment.
- Healthcare.
- Retail.

Virtual learning, in the public-school system along with college education classes is growing more popular as a direct result of social distancing guidelines in place in many jurisdictions.

Virtual classrooms are being created by many educational institutions and one example of a company benefitting from this evolution is Zoom (ZM). Zoom is one of several video communication companies seeing an uptick in use and popularity amongst businesses, governments, the performing arts and online education providers.

Businesses tapping into the online communication industry for educational and business purposes should do well over the coming years. There's a growing need for platforms capable of providing communication services for learning and sharing opportunities in fields once reserved to brick and mortar institutions. Teleconferencing is growing exponentially.

The movie and television industries have seen a radical shift in how they deliver movies and programming since the onset of the coronavirus. With movie theatres being closed, consumers gravitated to purchasing subscriptions to online content providers like Netflix (NFLX) and Roku (ROKU).

These online entertainment providers should see steady increases in viewership as more and more consumers hungry for entertainment stream online content. As well, movie studios are offering online rentals of recent releases while social distancing practices continue and consumer confidence wanes.

These subtle changes into how we consume entertainment will permeate the industry moving forward. Expect consumers to embrace using these platforms extensively in the "new normal" world.

Another radical change occurring as a result of the pandemic is in the healthcare sector. Telemedicine, whereby health providers offer one-on-one virtual consultations with a medical health professional is on the rise. Companies like Teladoc Health (TDOC) offer quick, affordable, and convenient access to medical assistance.

Within the health care sector, those businesses developing next generation gene and cell therapies, COVID-19 treatment therapies and vaccines will do well over the coming years. This pandemic is not going away any time soon. Expect global seasonal resurgences to occur until an effective, widely administered vaccine has been developed and distributed. Medical experts anticipate that this could take 18 to 24 months from testing to widespread inoculation to create herd immunity.

In the short-term companies manufacturing personal protection equipment, COVID-19 testing kits and high-tech items like ventilators or rapid-testing machines will do well over the next year as many jurisdictions rebuild equipment stockpiles in anticipation of future outbreaks.

In the retail sector, most mom and pop specialty shops, along with restaurants and bars have been hit the hardest. Most have been forced to close in the wake of the pandemic. This is also impacting mall operators who have seen their share prices plunge in the wake of store closures and fear in the markets. Consumer confidence will take time to return.

In non-food retail, consumer demand for major purchases or luxury consumer goods has dropped off, mainly due to concerns about contracting the virus, uncertainty about incomes, and the compulsory closure of many storefronts. In all likelihood, consumer demand for such items will remain depressed until most social distancing restrictions are eased.

Expect to see these main societal changes as social and economic restrictions are slowly lifted in 2020:

- An increase in online shopping habits.
- More people taking staycations or vacations in their local area.
- Restaurants and bars establishing stricter social distancing measures.
- More people working from home or remotely.
- Increased demand for at-home online entertainment options.
- Lower demand for most forms of transportation, public and private.

When it comes to investing in the stock market, these new realities provide you with some incredible opportunities. Opportunities abound. Knowing which one's are presenting themselves at a particular moment in time is the challenge. Let's address this concern right now.

Are there exceptions to the rule?

Despite many industries being decimated in the wake of the novel coronavirus outbreak, there are many exceptions to the rule within these highly susceptible industries.

True, it may take some time for live events to enjoy the audiences they once did. However, the live entertainment industry should look pretty much the same as it did before the pandemic.

Airlines were hurting during the pandemic, which is understandable as fewer individuals were flying for business and virtually no consumers were travelling for vacation purposes. Despite the downturn in passenger travel, air freight was at a premium. The movement of medical supplies and certain foodstuffs increased dramatically during the same period of consumer air travel contraction.

The transport and logistics industries should experience some catch up demand as international goods having been stuck along supply chains resume delivery. Lower fuel costs will weigh heavily in the rapid recovery of these industries.

In the retail sector, the Walmart's, Costco's and Targets of the retail world have fared better than most retailers. Fortunately, they're able to provide low-cost necessities to price-conscious consumers, who for the most part shop for food items and necessities.

Changing shopper habits have forced many brick-and-mortar retailers to quickly adapt to the online shopping world. Amazon has experienced increasing overall demand as consumers switch buying habits from shopping local to ordering online. Retail businesses ramping up online shopping and at-home delivery, should see a continued surge as consumer habits evolve over time.

Which industries should be the least affected?

We've identified the BEACH industries as being the most affected and challenged in bouncing back from recent downturns in the stock market. On the flip side, those industries that should be least affected include:

- Agriculture.
- Business services.
- Construction.

Although certain sections or aspects of the agricultural industry will be negatively impacted by the pandemic, people still need to eat. As social distancing restrictions ease and restaurants re-open, pre-coronavirus food supply chains will be reinstated.

The biggest current challenge within the overall industry is the labor shortage caused by travel restrictions impeding the movement of seasonal workers. You also have the temporary impact on certain sectors of the industry being affected when large numbers of food processing plant employees test positive for the virus and end up being sidelined for several weeks. All in all, agriculture should bounce back relatively quickly compared to other sectors of the economy.

Those businesses providing support services should remain relatively robust during the recession. Many of these businesses are able to continue operations with a significant portion of their workforce working from home. Companies like Zoom Video Communications (ZM) and Cisco (CSCO), which owns Webex one of the world's top collaboration platforms, have experienced explosive growth since the start of the pandemic-driven, work-from-home movement.

The construction industry should also be minimally impacted by the pandemic. As long as the economic devastation doesn't cause the massive postponement of new business premise construction, the industry should bounce back. Fortunately, most of the industry doesn't rely heavily on imports, nor on having to export goods. Supply chain disruption should be minimal for most construction businesses in North America.

COVID-19 will be with us for a long period of time. Until we can inoculate a large portion of the population with an effective vaccine, the virus will continue to disrupt our lives and impact the economy. Those industries learning how to co-exist with the novel coronavirus should bounce back faster than those not being able to adapt to the "new normal".

Now that you have a better idea as to what the business cycle looks like and how the current downturn in the stock market is affecting various industries, it's time to explore how you could find specific stocks poised to explode in the new economy. What follows in the next chapter are the steps to take in finding those rapidly growing businesses well-suited for momentum plays. I don't want to see you sitting around like a potted plant. Time to roll up your sleeves and hunker down.

4

HOW DO YOU FIND MOMENTUM STOCKS?

THE LAST CHAPTER put the current stock market crash into perspective. We glimpsed at how various industries might be affected by the global pandemic and ensuing economic meltdown in the markets. Now it's time to explore which industries and companies have a high probability of quickly rebounding and be potential candidates for momentum plays.

But the economic landscape has radically changed in 2020. No longer can we assume that it'll be business as usual once we get over the pandemic and economic downturn. How we go about conducting our lives has changed at a fundamental level.

Knowing what those changes are and integrating these insights into the stock selection process, opens up the possibility of finding great momentum stock plays.

Let's provide you with those insights that'll change how you think about big business in the future.

What has changed in the stock selection process?

What worked before the COVID-19 pandemic as far as finding potential momentum plays, won't work as effectively in our "new normal" society. The smart investor takes these new societal norms into account when looking for potential stock picks. And you want to be a smart investor.

The global pandemic caused two major societal changes. The first was seeing governments around the world imposing self-isolation or stay-at-home guidelines and orders. This effectively shut down most of the global economy in the wake of the growing pandemic. The second was the addition of social distancing guidelines for the general public in an attempt to limit the spread of the disease.

As a result of these unprecedented changes to the fabric of our society, businesses are adapting to a new way of conducting their affairs. Workplace and societal trends are evolving and a new normal is being established.

Many businesses are asking employees to work from home. Ecommerce is being favoured over brick and mortar establishments. More people are opting to use drive through services and home delivery as opposed to going out into the community.

Those businesses making it easier for consumers to adapt to these new realities can potentially be good momentum plays. As part of your selection criteria, you should integrate these insights into any selection process you decide to adopt. But before we look specifically at where to look for fast-growing companies, let's address one important concept beforehand.

How does herd immunity affect the stock market?

A return to some semblance of normalcy in the workplace is the number one concern of most Americans. Many people are fearful of catching COVID-19 out in public and eventually succumbing to the virus. Unfortunately, this novel coronavirus will be with us for a lengthy period of time.

Many health experts expect several waves of outbreak to occur over the next two years until herd immunity or protection is achieved. So, what is herd immunity and how does it affect what is transpiring in the economy?

First off, herd immunity happens when a certain level of the population become immune to the disease stopping its spread in the community. This can be achieved in two ways:

1. When a large percentage of the population contracts the virus and in time builds up a natural immunity to the disease.
2. The population is vaccinated against the disease to achieve immunity.

Health experts believe that 80 to 95 percent of the population needs to be immune to COVID-19 to stop its spread dead in its tracks. We're a long way off from achieving this level of immunity. So, in the meantime while we develop a reliable vaccine and see natural immunity to the disease develop, the global economy will be impacted.

What does this mean for you - the budding stock investor? Expect some level of disruption in the stock market over the next year or two. If you're a "buy, hold and pray my stock will go up" passive investor, this volatility in the markets will try your patience. If you're actively monitoring and trading momentum stocks, lucrative opportunities will appear more frequently over the coming years.

The global economy will eventually bounce back. You want to be positioned to take advantage of those rebounds when certain industries and businesses do take off. If anything, the upcoming months may prove to be some of the most opportune times to invest in fast-growing companies that have adapted well to a changed society where social distancing is the new norm.

Before looking at which industries to avoid and those to embrace over the coming months, let's outline how the selection process of finding potential growth plays fits into an overall approach for momentum investing. There's not much point in talking about various aspects of the stock investment process if you don't have a basic understanding of how the process unfolds.

How do you narrow down you stock picks?

Once you have an idea as to where to look for potential fast-growing businesses to invest in, it's time to narrow down your choices to just a handful of options. We want the entire process to be as painless as possible. And what do I mean by that?

Momentum investing has the distinct advantage of being less research intensive as compared to other investment approaches such as value or even income investing. Fewer selection criteria are necessary in order to evaluate fast-growing businesses.

With fewer fundamental financial indicators and

technical indicators from stock chart analysis being required to find and assess the growth potential of businesses, it becomes a much easier process to follow. Easy peasy is what we want.

Simplicity in finding, assessing, strategizing and timing market plays is a primary focus of this guide. This can be achieved by following a 3-step approach, as follows:

1. Screen for stocks using four main fundamental indicators and creating a watchlist of potential candidates.
2. Look for specific investment candidates using four stock chart technical indicators. Monitor this watchlist for developments and timely investment opportunities.
3. Complete your due diligence before investing by verifying whether or not the company's management team and the momentum within the stock market are on your side.

I realize researching potential investment candidates can be about as exciting as cooking broccoli or boiling potatoes. However, it need not be an onerous task, if we keep it simple.

Time to narrow down your choices as to which industries would logically benefit from the current economic landscape. Let's start by excluding industries who'll be affected the longest.

Which industries will be slower to recover? And why?

Any industry relying on mass gatherings of customers or patrons will be slow to recover until herd immunity is achieved. Granted, in the interim many of these industries where the masses gather are going to adapt to social distancing guidelines. The challenge moving forward for many of these industries is reassuring consumers and building their confidence so more people return to these industries.

Some of the businesses and industries that could experience a slower recovery are movie theatres, cruises, amusement parks, shopping malls, sporting events, live concerts, and convention centres.

Until a vaccine has been developed and we see widespread herd immunity appear, these business models whereby masses gather, will be slow to recover. Sure, there will be exceptions to the rule, especially with businesses capable of adapting to social distancing guidelines.

Right now, we want to avoid these industries in the short term until we see a shift in societal behavior back to a life resembling what society experienced prior to the pandemic. Once we see a relaxing of social distancing measures along with a return of consumer confidence in going out into society, we'll begin to see these industries ramp up and take off. This would be a more opportune time to consider momentum plays for these specific businesses.

Which industries will bounce back quickly? And why?

According to Bill Gates in an April 26 CNN television interview, the technology sector is poised the best to recover the fastest from the recession. He goes on to say that the economic recovery will be slow as parts of the economy open up over the course of 2020 and we experience lower economic outputs. Those sectors seeing a relatively fast recovery will be education, manufacturing and construction, as previously mentioned.

Specific to the technology sector, companies using blockchain technology have great growth potential. Blockchain uses cryptology and timestamps to build secure, stable, digital ledgers used in the health care, financial, retail and manufacturing industries. Many analysts are predicting an annualized growth rate of 35 percent over the next five consecutive years. Imagine where you might be at when you couple these enviable growth rates with a rebound in the overall market. Makes me as giddy as a four-year old in a candy store.

Along with advances in blockchain development, growth in artificial intelligence applications by cloud-based applications and services is unfolding. Two areas of note are developments in AI-powered industrial robots and natural language processing for customer service applications. As for robotics, most people understand this application of technology in the workplace. Natural language processing may be harder to visualize. When you think of natural language processing, think of voice recognition and processing by AI applications like Siri, Google Assistant and Alexa. This is another industry the analysts are expecting to generate a 30 percent annualized return over the next seven years.

On the manufacturing front, in the short-term those businesses manufacturing medical supplies and drug therapies should benefit from the pandemic. Your investigation into potential momentum plays should include pharmaceuticals involved in developing a COVID-19 vaccine. Or, check out companies developing testing systems and supplies.

So, where do you go from here?

. . .

Where should you be looking for these prospects?

Start by using the Internet to do some preliminary investigation. Initially, look for businesses that profit from the primary cause of a sell-off in the markets. In other words, our current recession was triggered by the global pandemic; therefore, look to those businesses who would profit from remedying or mitigating the situation. You're looking for the catalyst triggering the economic meltdown.

Based on this analysis, some businesses to explore would be medical suppliers of personal protective equipment, ventilators, testing equipment and supplies. These businesses should see rapid growth in sales over the course of 2020 as demand surges at all levels of the government, within industries, and by the general public.

The next step is to look for anomalies within industries. Businesses are getting very innovative as to how they're conducting operations. Those businesses coming out on top will be the ones adapting the quickest to the "new normal". This positions them better for a faster rebound, especially when Mr. Market embraces their innovation and rewards them with increased valuations in the stock market.

Examples of positive developments occurring in certain industries would be some of the following:

- **Entertainment:** Renting new movie releases from home versus seeing movies on the big screen.
- **Food service:** Offering gourmet food take out versus brick and mortar restaurant dining.
- **Health & Fitness:** In-home fitness options versus going to the local gym.
- **Education:** Online remote education versus attending schools and colleges.

Finally, use the tools and resources currently available in the marketplace to get ideas as to industries and businesses that show promise. Three of my favorite sources are:

1. Heat map apps identifying stocks showing rapid growth like StockTouch, MarketCarpet or Finviz.
2. News feeds from sources like: Motley Fool's Stock Advisor, TheStreet, Investor's Business Daily or Investopedia.
3. Stock investing publications like: Smart Investor, The 100 Best Aggressive Stocks, or How to Make Money in Stocks.

All of these resources should get you thinking about those businesses having the potential for rapid growth coming out of this current recession. You should also be in a better position to capitalize on future downturns in the market knowing you can access tools that'll make it easier to find great momentum plays.

Now that you have a better idea as to which industries and businesses to explore, let's take a more detailed look at what makes a good stock pick for momentum plays.

HOW TO ANALYZE PROSPECTS

FINDING and assessing stocks for momentum plays uses a combination of fundamental and technical indicators. Fundamental indicators are those metrics tied to the financial health and profitability of a business. Technical indicators use the power of visual representation and analytical tools found in graphing and charting to provide insights into how a stock is evolving over time in the stock market.

Key to the overall assessment process is keeping the entire process as simple and easy to use and understand as possible. We also want to have an evaluation process requiring as few indicators as possible to achieve the desired results for both momentum and option plays. This can be accomplished with as few as four fundamental and four technical indicators. Contrast this with some stock market approaches requiring upwards of a dozen indicators. Can you imagine how much time and frustration a simple assessment approach will save you?

The momentum strategies used during a market rebound when coupled with covered call option strategies offer the best overall growth potential. We'll tackle covered call writing in Chapter 7. Right now, let's focus on providing you with a simple momentum strategy that's easy to implement.

How do you initially screen for momentum prospects?

When you're initially screening for potential momentum plays and placing candidates on a watchlist for further investigation, it may help to quickly weed out many stocks by using two main criteria. One is a fundamental indicator that looks at the annual growth rate of company revenues. The other is a technical indicator seen on stock charts for assessing stock price appreciation over time.

Your overall goal is to identify those businesses with a high probability of experiencing rapid-stock price appreciation. You're looking for businesses that will quickly rebound from any recession and also show substantial revenue growth rate, hopefully over the course of a year or two. This enables you to benefit from stock price appreciation along with monthly income generation from selling covered call options on stock you are holding over the course of the year.

These two initial screening indicators are:

1. Annual revenue growth rate > 15 percent (fundamental).
2. 50-day Simple Moving Average > 200-day Simple Moving Average (technical).

Most financial websites report revenue or sales growth rates for companies listed on a stock exchange. What's important to understand when looking at any financial or technical data is to focus on the rate of change the data is reporting, not the raw numbers.

For example, a value of 200 points looks like a lot on the computer screen for the Dow Jones Industrial Average for any one day. The raw data looks impressive. However, if the DOW is sitting at 25,000 points, then this daily change only represents less than a 1 percent change, which is not a huge rate of change.

No matter which fundamental indicator you're using, always lean towards those expressing the rate of change. The rate of change of any financial indicator allows you to easily compare like businesses together.

The same holds true of using technical indicators found on stock charts.

In an ideal world, you want to see the sales or revenue growth rate above 15 percent each year over a three-year period of time. Coming out of a major recession or prolonged stock market meltdown may prove more challenging to deal with in the assessment process. Don't discount a company just because revenues have dropped below 15 percent in and around a recessionary period. The company may still be a viable investment opportunity upon further investigation.

Use the revenue growth rate to initially screen for top performing stocks having the potential to grow rapidly as the economy turns around. Consider placing potential candidates on a "watchlist" so you can apply additional elimination criteria to the mix in order to come up with a shortlist of fast-growing companies.

The second indicator to use for initially screening watchlist candidates, is when the 50-day simple moving average crosses above the 200-day simple moving average. Moving averages are calculated by taking the arithmetic mean (average) of stock prices over a set period of time. For a 50-day simple moving average, closing stock prices over a 50-day period of time are used to calculate an average value, which is then plotted along a line on a technical chart. Having an average, smooths out price trends by filtering out random short-term swings.

When the 50-day average moves above the 200-day average, you're seeing share price growth. These two graph lines are often set as the default setting for many technical charts. And where can you find these charts? Great question my astute investing machine apprentice. All online brokerage accounts provide charting technology, as do websites like StockCharts.com.

Armed with just these two indicators, you should be able to generate a watchlist of growth plays to explore further. Depending on how enthusiastic and motivated you are in conducting an initial stock search, you should try to create a list of at least 20 possibilities. Doing so, allows you to eventually eliminate low-yielding prospects and still have several investment prospects to monitor.

Your watchlist need not be elaborate. It could be a notebook containing basic information about the stock being investigated along with some key metrics and dates as to when you compiled or updated any data. You could also set up a table or chart within an electronic spreadsheet to keep track of developments. This seems to be the best option when you factor in how easy it is to update any findings on a particular business over time.

How should you assess the profitability of each candidate?

Once you've identified a number of investment candidates, it's time to assess the profitability of each candidate. What you're looking for are those businesses having the greatest upside potential for stock price appreciation. We want stocks that'll grow like those wire coat hangers accumulating in your closet.

This can be accomplished by first using a handful of financial indicators to assess the growth potential of the business and then by looking at a few technical indicators to determine if the stock market concurs.

The main advantage of using such a simple approach, is the time it'll save you during the screening and selection process for potential momentum plays. Keeping track of just a few parameters cuts down on the work involved in creating your watchlist.

When you contrast this with the traditional approach to assessing businesses by looking at:

- upwards of a dozen fundamental indicators over a 3 to 5-year time span, then

- determining the type and extent of a competitive advantage the business has, followed by
- assessing the management team's focus and fair compensation,

you can appreciate following a simpler approach. The fewer hoops you have to jump through to arrive at an investment candidate, the less frustrating and time intensive the whole process. I'm sure you have better things to do with your time rather than having to spend hours analyzing possibilities.

No need to spend hours on end analyzing financial statements. Should you decide to delve deeper into the financials of a company, they do provide you with beneficial insights. Financials are like a bikini. What they reveal is interesting and what they conceal is vital to your understanding of the stock as being an investment possibility.

Businesses come into favour and fall out of favour with Mr. Market all the time. For several months, you may see investors pouring money into a certain stock. Institutional investors may have jumped on the band wagon and look favourably on a particular holding as being a good investment. Upward stock price momentum is creating demand for the stock.

So, how do we tap into these scenarios whereby you can use just a handful of indicators for selecting these profitable momentum stocks?

Let's look at the fundamental and technical indicators to use in more detail.

Which fundamental indicators are the most helpful?

In order to identify a stock as having upside growth potential, you'll want to focus your attention on the following four basic parameters:

1. Strong current sales growth being greater than 15 percent.
2. Strong return on invested capital also being greater than 15 percent.
3. Strong future earnings projections. EPS growth over the next 5 years should indicate a positive trend.
4. The stock has a history of beating analyst quarterly earnings estimates.

1. Revenue Growth Rate:

The revenue or sales growth rate takes a look at the total amount of money the business took in from selling its products and/ or services. The raw number can be found on the top line of the income statement for the company. However, we're more concerned with the rate of change in revenue growth year-over-year. Increasing profitability is what we're looking for.

When exploring this parameter, look at the prospect's revenue growth over a 1-year, 2-year and 3-year timeframe. Double-digit growth rates are what you're looking for. Ideally, shoot for an annual growth rate above 15 percent. Many financial websites and your online brokerage account will have screening tools that'll allow you to narrow down your list of prospects.

2. Return on Invested Capital Growth Rate:

Along with revenue growth, we would like the business to be able to receive a rate of return off of the cash it generates. This is known as the Return on Invested Capital (ROIC). The beauty of this metric is that it's already providing you with the rate of change. No need to use any initial raw data to calculate this value.

This metric tells you how effective the business is in using its own and borrowed money to generate a return. It also indicates how effective the business is in using invested capital to grow the business.

As above, look for patterns of ROIC growth over three years being in the double digits, with the most recent year approaching 15 percent. This metric coupled with the revenue growth rate helps predict future stock growth by indicating how increasing revenues are being allocated and invested.

3. Earnings Per Share Growth Rate:

When you're a shareholder in a business, you want to see growth in your equity. The Earnings Per Share (EPS) indicates how much profit the business generates per share of ownership. This raw number is found along the last line on the business's income statement. We're more concerned about the growth rate moving forward. Look for analyst projections as to the EPS growth rate over the next 5 years. A positive growing trend in EPS growth increases the probability of finding a profitable holding.

4. Quarterly Analyst Earnings Estimates.

Mr. Market looks favourably upon those businesses consistently beating analyst estimates as to earnings growth. Many institutional investors consider pumping additional capital into stocks showing better than estimated earnings growth. This upward trend in momentum is exactly what you're looking for. Your online brokerage platform should have this data readily available for you to check out.

As you can see, these four parameters need not be a time-consuming, all-encompassing analytical process to undertake. In fact, each parameter requires a minimum of time to analyze, yet packs a punch in terms of valuable insights into the growth of a business.

Which fundamental indicators are less helpful?

Some criteria helpful in identifying those businesses that are undervalued and showing promising growth over a long time period are not as helpful as the four parameters previously discussed.

Should you be conservative in your investment approach and wanting to invest in solid mature companies paying out a quarterly dividend, then looking at the dividend payout ratio is a useful metric. Likewise, the Debt-to-Equity Ratio is a great indicator of how much debt a business is carrying. If there is a great deal of debt, dividends may be slashed in order to ensure paying off bond holders first.

The same holds true of the Equity or Book Value Per Share (BVPS) metric, which tells you what the business would be worth if it were to liquidate. Businesses growing their equity over time and not spending excessive funds to build capital-intensive projects tend to be more mature, steady growers. Not exactly what we're looking for in a rapidly growing younger company looking to expand production and revenues.

As you can see, all of these metrics provide useful insights into how a business grows over time. What you need to focus on are those metrics which will provide you with some of the best insights into how to use a momentum approach to stock investing. Revenue and earnings drive most markets in the short term. This is where you want to be in your analysis.

Which technical indicators are the most helpful?

As previously mentioned, both the 50-day simple moving average and the 200-day simple moving average are helpful in assessing momentum. You used these two technical indicators in your initial screening. Recall a 50-day MA above the 200-day MA indicates share price appreciation.

Besides looking at trends in stock price changes over time, there are three other technical parameters to integrate into the overall selection process. Not only are these technicals helpful in assessing potential momentum opportunities, but you'll also use these same parameters in order to help assess potential options plays for income production from your holdings.

The other three basic technical parameters you need to track are:

1. The volume of shares being traded over a period of several months.
2. Whether or not the stock is oversold or under bought using the Relative Stock Index (RSI).
3. What momentum trend is occurring for the stock using the Moving Average Convergence Divergence graph (MACD).

1. Volume.

The volume of shares being traded on a daily basis is often shown at the bottom of a technical chart as a series of histograms or bars. An increasing volume of transactions for a given time period coupled with rising share prices, indicates positive momentum for that stock.

Monitoring patterns in volume growth or decline in relation to share price appreciations helps predict potential growth. Start by comparing the average 10-day volume to the average 3-month volume. When 10-day volume increases above the 3-month volume, a buy signal can often be triggered as stock price momentum is on your side.

2. Relative Strength Index (RSI).

The Relative Strength Index measure the speed and magnitude of directional price movement in a stock. It uses a scale from 0 to 100, with high and low levels typically marked at 80 and 20, respectively. RSI values above 80 usually indicate a stock is entering a period of being over bought and buyers may reverse the trend by selling shares. The opposite is true for a value of 20, which indicates an under bought state of affairs with investors looking at pouring money back into share purchases should the business have solid fundamentals.

As a momentum investor, look for situations where the RSI is above 50, yet below 80, when looking at investing. Stocks purchased in this sweet zone have a greater chance of delivering. The same holds true of option plays for the stock in question.

3. Moving Average Convergence Divergence (MACD).

The Moving Average Convergence Divergence is a technical indicator used to help predict when a momentum trend is beginning or ending. The indicator is composed of two moving average lines as well as a zero line. By plotting changes to each line on a technical chart, we can use the predictive properties of the indicator to help assess if a momentum trend is reversing.

The easiest way to use this indicator is to look at it in bar chart form. A bar chart above the zero line tends to indicate a positive or bullish trend. A bar chart falling below the zero line, leans toward a more bearish or slower momentum outlook.

To increase this tool's sensitivity, change the default setting of 12, 26, 9 to 8, 17, 9. This setting is helpful when looking at shorter periods of time, as well as for options plays.

So far, we've identified four fundamental and four technical indicators you'll use to select momentum stocks that also have options trading possibilities. Now, it's time to look at the specific buy and sell criteria to adhere to when using a momentum trading approach.

Once you have a better understanding as to the rules of engagement and why they're set up this way, we'll tackle generating additional monthly income with the sale of covered calls in the following chapter.

What buy signals should you be looking for?

So far, you've created a watchlist of potential momentum plays using the moving averages and revenue growth rate as screening criteria. Now, it's time to apply each of the other six criteria to the analytical process.

What you're attempting to do is identify those stocks that are in favour with Mr. Market and are showing accelerated growth in the stock market. You're trying to capture significant gains in stock price appreciation over a relatively short period of time, which could be several months long to a couple of years depending on the industry and business's growth potential.

After you've created an initial watchlist, you'll want to narrow down your investment choices to just a handful of fast-growing stocks. Use the remaining selection criteria to evaluate each candidate. What you're looking at doing is selecting and then prioritizing the best possibilities.

Not every stock will show up as being an immediate momentum play as you examine each business using the selection criteria. Some businesses may require more time to get the "go ahead" signal for investment. Just keep monitoring these future possibilities over time.

To give you an idea as to what your ideal candidate looks like, here are the 8 assessment criteria in a nutshell:

1. Revenue growth > 15 percent per annum.
2. ROIC > 10 to 15 percent per annum.
3. EPS forward 5-year growth rate is positive.
4. Stock beats analyst's quarterly earnings estimates.
5. 50-day MA > 200-day MA.
6. 10-day volume > 3-month volume.

7. RSI between 50 and 80.
8. MACD above zero line.

When all of these stars magically line up, you have a higher probability of coming out on top in your momentum plays. This analysis is not sexy. You're not going to turn to your grandmother and say, "Hey baba Ho-Tep, doesn't this turn your crank?" However, the process does increase you level of confidence in potential momentum plays.

What's the best approach to purchasing your stocks?

When you're ready to purchase shares of stock, you'll be presented with two buying options once you log into your online broker platform. If you would like to pick up the shares at the current market value, enter a "market" order on your platform. The order should be filled at the current stock price within minutes of placing the request.

However, if you feel you could purchase the shares at a price slightly below the currently listed stock price, enter a "limit" order. A limit order sets the maximum amount you would like to spend for those shares of stock. Since the stock market is an actively traded market, share prices fluctuate throughout the day.

You'll notice when you want to purchase shares of stock for any equity, your trading platform will display a "bid" and an "ask" price. The bid price is what you and other buyers would like to purchase the shares for. This value is always lower than the ask price. The ask price is what sellers of the stock would like to receive for unloading their shares.

The "mid-point" price is found between the bid and ask prices. By setting a limit order between the mid-point and the lower bid price, you can often purchase your shares for slightly less than the current market value displayed. This approach can work well when some volatility is occurring during trading and you're patient enough to wait for your limit order to be filled.

Can you time the market?

There are more favourable times during the trading day and week whereby you can purchase shares of stock. In order to make the connection between what price you'll pay for your stock and the best times to enter the market, we need to get into the mindset of the investors on the others side of the transaction.

Take for example Monday mornings. Many institutional investors, who coincidentally drive the markets, return to work with emotional baggage. They may or may not have spent an enjoyable relaxing weekend with friends and family. Once in the so-called "trading pits", they sometimes let emotions more than logic rule out.

The markets and your stock may experience increased price volatility until trader's emotions dissipate. Although you can pick up stocks at a discount by being as nimble as a ninja warrior, a better approach is to wait until emotions have coursed through the markets and they're trading less on emotion. Sitting on the sidelines on Monday can often be the best strategy when picking up shares of stock.

Another day to avoid might be Friday's. The stock market often experiences increased volatility for whatever reason on Fridays. Many institutional buyers unload their holdings just before the weekend. They prefer not holding onto any volatile stocks or those that may be affected by weekend news reports.

You may also experience low trading volume near the end of the day on Fridays as many professional traders take off work early. What this means is that retail investors or smaller players tend to temporarily move the markets. Rising stock prices coupled with low volume equates to an unsustainable trend. It's more prudent to sidestep the markets until after the weekend.

So, when might be better days for popping into the stock market? Wednesdays and Thursdays can often prove to be the ideal days for picking up shares.

As to times of the day to avoid. The markets tend to be

more volatile at the opening bell. Wait at least an hour to see how they're reacting. You don't want to overpay for your positions. Also keep in mind, most markets trade in the Eastern Time Zone; therefore, take this into account depending on where you live.

Another problematic time is the lunch hour as many institutional buyers head off to lunch. With fewer traders, stock volume can lag not giving you the full picture as to the direction the markets are heading. Be patient. Wait until the end of the day when volume tends to be the heaviest to assess your timing opportunity to buy.

Now that you have a good idea as to how to pick up momentum stocks using a handful of fundamental indicators, technical charts and timing strategies, let's look at when you should exit your stock positions. Keep in mind, you want to follow a system which is simple and easy to implement. It should be easy peasy.

WHEN SHOULD YOU EXIT YOUR STOCK POSITIONS

You now know under what parameters to use in moving into momentum plays. Just a handful of indicators are needed to assess whether or not a stock has potential for upward mobility of its price. And, you also can better time moving into the market when Mr. Market is behind you.

Now, it's time to determine under what conditions you need to exit any momentum position.

What exit strategies do you need to adhere to?

A momentum trading approach to stock investing does come with greater risk of capital loss in comparison to value investing or dividend investing approaches. It also comes with a higher probability of significant stock price appreciation compared to these more conservative approaches. Knowing that the risk of capital loss is greater, we need to have a capital protection system in place that:

1. Has simple exit signals triggering the sale of a particular holding.
2. Ensures we don't have excessive exposure of our capital in one holding.
3. Minimizes the erosion of overall returns by excessive transaction fees.
4. Allows us to reduce our losses by selling call options on our holdings.

When you take on the role of being a do-it-yourself investor you accept the responsibility of monitoring your holdings on a regular basis. Most do-it-yourself investors check into their online discount brokerage platforms at least once a day. Taking a few minutes each day isn't a huge time commitment yet provides you with some peace of mind knowing you're keeping tabs on your positions.

We'll address how to best develop your winning edge in the markets in the last chapter. Suffice it to say, the mental aspect of investing plays a significant role into how successful you'll be as a stock investor. Knowing how to tap into this effectively will set you apart from most investors. Hope is not a solid investment strategy.

When you live on hope it's like living on a 500 calorie-a-day diet.

1. Holding to simple exit signals.

Let's explore each of the four factors in detail, starting with having a set of simple exit signals for minimizing capital loss. There are three signals to keep an eye on when monitoring your holdings.

Trigger #1: Sell, if the current stock price drops 15 percent from your purchase price.

Most investors reel at the thought of experiencing huge losses in the stock market, especially when many such scenarios can be prevented. Too many investors are so set in their ways as a chunk of concrete, not willing to take precautions. Letting the market happen to you is like being in a comfortable bed; easy to get into but harder to get out of.

The easiest way to exit the market when your stock price is dropping is with a "stop-loss" order. A stop-loss order is a set of automatic instructions you set up with your online broker to sell your position when the stock price drops to a set price. This can be done with either a percentage drop from the original purchase price or a fixed stock price.

Setting a stop-loss order at 15 percent of your entry price limits your losses. Using a wide 15 percent stop-loss allows for wider natural swings in the market, especially with momentum stocks. By setting a narrow stop loss of 5 percent, you do limit your losses better; however, you also run the risk of being taken out of the market due to the natural volatility in the markets on any particular trading day.

Trigger #2: Sell, if the 50-day MA closes below the 200-day MA.

When the moving day averages on a technical chart show the stock trading on lower and lower stock prices, it's time to pull the plug. The upward trend is now over and in all likelihood momentum in the markets for that holding is moving in a negative direction.

Your best bet in this scenario is to exit the market. Sell your shares and take any profits off the table. You can always enter the market with another momentum play once you've cashed in.

Trigger #3: Sell, if the stock rises 300 percent from your purchase price.

Although this is a rare occurrence in the stock market, it happens more often than not with stocks trading on momentum after a significant stock market correction. You've benefitted from a significant increase in the stock's price. It's time to look for the next momentum play.

To quickly calculate what a 300 percent exit price would be for any stock, just multiple your original purchase price by 4.

You may be wondering why these somewhat arbitrary numbers of 15 percent and 300 percent were chosen. Why not 10 and 200 percent? Good question, my intuitive padawan.

The basic assumption being made is you'll risk 15 percent of your capital to make 300 percent. When you do the math, one winning trade pays for 20 losing trades, which is a super risk-reward ratio. Put another way, if you had to exit your positions 90 percent of the time, you could still expect a 15 percent return over the long term within your stock portfolio. Not a bad scenario.

Granted, this hypothetical scenario is based on having one stock hit a home run for you while all your other holdings turn to mush. Both situations of knocking the ball out of the park at the same time as being kicked to the curb twenty times are highly unlikely to unfold. What's important to understand is creating a favourable risk-reward ratio.

For illustrative purposes, you could use a 10 percent

and 200 percent ratio between risk and reward. The 200 percent exit point is psychologically easier to wrap your brain around when looking at potential growth. It's a much more realistic goal to achieve than 300 percent. I'll give you that.

Here you would be willing to lose up to 10 percent in order to make 200. The difficulty with this model, is in the implementation. It's not uncommon for stock prices to whip-saw down more than 10 percent only to rebound back an equal amount over the course of a trading session.

Should you have set a stop-loss order at 10 percent, this means you would have been taken out of the market. What's even more frustrating is having this happen and then seeing the stock price shoot for the stars on good news with an earnings report, new technological advancement or other positive development.

It's important to understand the underlying premise behind each of these scenarios. Strive to reduce your risk of capital loss, while exploiting the upside potential of riding momentum stocks higher when Mr. Market is on your side. This brings the discussion to the next inter-related topic of determining how big each position should be.

2. Limiting risk with small positions.

So, the question now becomes: How much capital should I risk for any particular trade when using a momentum approach to investing?

You can imagine all investment gurus are all over the map on this one. Some of the most successful investors keep their trades as small as 2 percent of their overall portfolio value. This approach reduces portfolio risk immensely as a major loss typically has a small effect on the overall portfolio value. Unfortunately, most novice investors or those rebounding from a stock market meltdown, don't have enormous investment portfolios to play with.

A more reasonable expectation is to invest no more than 15 percent of your total portfolio into any one opportunity. Depending on your personal risk tolerance level, you may wish to limit your exposure even more. In which case, a 10 percent limit might be more palatable in the event of an unforeseen catastrophic loss.

Let's put everything you've touched on so far into perspective with a concrete example. Assume you have $16,000 in your trading accounts. If you're just starting out, it may make sense to try and spread your capital evenly amongst 8 to 10 picks. This would mean allocating up to $2000 for each buy signal giving you a minimum of 8 potential holdings or 12.5 percent of your overall portfolio per allocation.

In the event you're forced to exit any one position with a 15 percent stop-loss, you would experience a $200 loss (not including transaction fees) or 1.25 percent of your trading portfolio. This is a manageable loss. It's not as if you'll be forced to sell everything and move back into your parent's basement should this situation occur.

On the flip side, when you adopt a momentum investment approach you should expect a potential 15 percent annualized return. The parameters used to screen for good momentum stock picks took revenue, capital and earnings growth into consideration. And since momentum investing benefits the most when markets are rebounding out of a recession or major market correction, you have a lot of upside potential to tap into.

3. Limiting transaction fees.

Gains made in the stock market can quickly be eroded by transaction fees. Take for example, actively traded mutual funds, which often charge management expense ratios (MER's) around 2 to 3 percent. These are fees charged by the mutual fund company to manage your holdings. Should you have a mutual fund generating an annualized return of 9 percent, your portfolio is taking a significant hit to the bottom line.

For example, a 3 percent MER taken off the top represents a 33 percent decrease in your overall portfolio growth, not just 3 percent. The MER represents 1/3 of your overall growth (9 percent less 3 percent leaves you with 6 percent).

Why bring this up? Fees eat away at your overall profitability. Pay attention as to how much you'll be paying. And it all starts with setting up an appropriate trading platform.

Most large brick-and-mortar financial institutions offering brokerage services tend to charge more for using their trading platforms. I can remember the day when trading options cost me about $100 per transaction.

Fast forward to today and you can find brokers who'll gladly accept less than $10 per transaction. In the fall of 2019, brokers waged a price war on transaction fees for both equities and options, which you can expect to continue throughout 2020. Most brokers offer no or very minimal transaction fees. What has evolved in the online world is the nature of doing business. No longer do you need offices in every major city. Online business costs have dropped substantially. And that's good news for you.

To reduce your transaction fees for both buying and selling equities, along with selling option contracts, consider using the services of an online discount broker. A quick Google search will identify those online brokers offering reasonable transaction fees, robust trading platforms and easy-to-access customer support. This is the route to go as a do-it-yourself stock investor.

Although it's highly unlikely, it is possible transaction fees could erode your gains when making multiple transactions over the course of a year. Being proactive and using the services of a discount broker will give you peace of mind and fewer headaches knowing fees won't be eating away at any gains being made.

As a rule of thumb, try to keep your transaction fees to less than 1 percent of your capital outlay. For example, if you're paying $10 in transaction fees for a small stock purchase, ensure you invest at least $1000.

Another consideration to take into account when you're purchasing a block of shares for your portfolio, is to purchase the shares in what is known as "round lots". Investors are used to buying and selling shares in even blocks of typically 100 shares of stock per block. Transaction fees can be kept to a minimum when you buy and sell shares in round lots.

Another important factor is should your stock pick

also trade in the options market, you can only sell (and buy) option contracts in round lots of 100. Each option contract controls 100 shares of stock. So, why not set yourself up from the get go with an ideal scenario?

4. Reducing risk by selling call options.

I've briefly alluded to using call options as an effective strategy to pair with trading momentum stocks. You'll discover the ins and outs of when and how to use these financial instruments in conjunction with stock holdings in the following chapters.

What's important to grasp, is that selling call options on stock you own cannot only create a monthly income stream for you down the road, but also protect your holdings from loss. Protecting your capital should be your number 1 priority when investing in the stock market.

To do so, you'll want to place more weight on those potential momentum stocks trading in the options market. Being able to tap into both stock price appreciation along with monthly income coming in from covered calls creates a more favourable risk-reward ratio.

This is why the eight indicators selected for assessing the merits of each stock pick have been selected. Not only do they provide you with some screening criteria as to momentum plays, but you can also use the same indicators to make well-informed decisions as to option plays.

When you use a momentum trading strategy, expect to occasionally incur losses. Being able to mitigate your losses with appropriate strategies becomes paramount to your success. In general, you'll want to focus on investing in stocks with high revenue growth.

This overall investment strategy is effective in rebounding markets. Not only do you profit from rapid risers but you're also in a position to side-step down markets. When the 50-day MA drops below the 200-day MA, it's a signal to sit on the sidelines with that particular equity. Upward momentum is slowing or even reversing, and it may be time to consider exiting your position, especially if you notice revenue growth stalling. Time to patiently sit in a cash position until the next awesome growth opportunity presents itself.

Keep in mind that the only time you make money in the stock market is when you actually cash in your holdings. Paper profits are just that. They hold no actual cash value until you actually pull the plug and sell your positions.

The opposite also holds true for you. Any time you look at your holdings within your online brokerage platform, you haven't lost or gained anything until you sell. Should you be caught in a market crash, it isn't the end of the story for your holdings. Markets do trend upward over time. Often solid companies being unfairly dragged down by the overall market, rapidly bounce back once confidence shifts. You want to wait patiently like a cat at a mouse hole.

To help protect your positions a little better and generate some additional cash in your brokerage account, let's explore the wonderful world of options trading. The next chapter walks you through the ins and outs of options, what they are and what four simple pieces of information you need to place any options trade.

COVERED CALL INVESTING BASICS

You're about to find out what covered calls are and how they can be used in conjunction with a momentum trading approach to protect your investment, as well as generate income.

Unlike most momentum trend investors, you have another tool you can draw upon from your arsenal of investment weapons. That weapon happens to be periodically using options contracts. However, before looking at the specific strategies to incorporate into your overall investment plan, we need to address a fundamental question.

What are covered calls?

The stock option market is set up for the purpose of buying and selling shares of stock at a specific price by a specific date. This fixes the price of the stock for the buyer, so they can purchase it at an agreed upon price, if the stock price reaches a specified price.

An option's value is dynamic. It changes according to the price of the stock. When the stock price rises, so does the option's price. As the stock drops in price, so too does the option follow suit.

Time is the critical factor in options trading. Option contracts exist for a specific period of time only. All monthly option contracts expire on the third Friday of each month. This day is known as "expiration Friday". It also means some months will be four weeks long, while others will be five weeks. Option premiums paid will reflect the time value associated with each 4 or 5-week period of time.

When the deadline passes, the option contract becomes worthless and ceases to exist. As a result of this relationship, the option's value decreases as the deadline approaches, reaching zero at expiration.

An "option contract" gives the buyer the right, but not the obligation, to buy (or sell) 100 shares of stock. Recall, whenever possible, you want to initially buy shares of stock in round lots of 100 so you can participate in the options market.

The two most common options are "calls" and "puts",

that can be either bought or sold. We're most interested in selling call options, hence the focus on this particular type of option contract only in our discussions. In exchange for a cash "premium", call options grant the owner (otherwise known as the buyer) of the contract the right to buy 100 shares of a company's stock.

As a seller of an option contract, you're paid this premium. It's immediately deposited into the seller's brokerage account when the buyer on the other side of the contract agrees to the premium price. All of this process happens seamlessly behind the scenes in the options market.

In all of the options strategies discussed, you'll be acting as the seller of call options on stock you own. When you sell option contracts on stock you own, you're known as a "writer" of covered calls. The term "covered calls" refers to being able to deliver the actual shares of stock you own to the buyer, if your contracts should get sold. The sale of your option contracts to the buyer is also known as "being exercised" or "assigned" and the stock is "being called away".

In contrast, a "naked call" means you won't have shares of stock to exchange in the event of the option contract being exercised. You would have to settle up with cash coming from your brokerage account. Since most online brokers don't want to take on the risk of you not having enough cash to settle your obligation, this level of options trading comes with strict cash balance restrictions and approvals. This scenario is something you won't have to worry about with this book's investment approach.

When you sell covered calls, the buyer on the other side of the options contract has the right to buy your shares at an agreed upon price, which is known as the "strike price". The buyer of an option contract can exercise this right anytime the stock price reaches the agreed upon strike price before markets close on expiration Friday.

At first glance, this may appear to be a losing proposition in that your stocks are sold on you. However, recall that you benefited from the option premiums being deposited into your brokerage account as soon as you sell your contracts. A properly structured option contract should generate a conservative monthly return of 2 to 3 percent, which is nothing to sneeze at.

You also benefit from any stock price appreciation should you sell an option contract with a strike price higher than the current value of the stock you're holding. We'll look at this specific scenario in more detail in the following chapter, as this is the most effective call option strategy to use with a momentum trading approach.

Which brings us to look at why you should consider selling option contracts as part of the overall momentum trading approach.

What are the pros and cons of selling call options?

Before we address what the primary objectives of using options trading with momentum stocks might be, it may be helpful to point out the major advantages and concerns. Selling covered calls is one of the most conservative approaches in options trading. It provides you with three distinct benefits, namely:

1. Creates monthly or bi-monthly income.

Selling covered calls on a monthly basis can generate a significant amount of additional income. A safe monthly option return expectation is in the range of 2 to 3 percent. This strategy alone can generate double-digit returns for your investment portfolio over the course of a year. Granted you won't be able to write covered calls every month. However, the annual income potential can be enticing.

When you sell option contracts the premium being paid to you is automatically deposited into your brokerage account at the beginning of the month in question. You now have the opportunity to use this cash injection for future stock purchases or transactions.

2. Reduces portfolio risk.

When you're paid a cash premium for selling each of your covered call contracts, this cash injection reduces your initial cost price or "cost basis" for your stock. The initial stock price is being reduced by the equivalent amount of premium deposited into your brokerage account.

Should the stock price decline below your initial price paid, it would have to drop by the amount of premium being deposited before impacting your capital outlay. In other words, your breakeven point for the stock is lowered by your option premium. This builds in a margin of safety into preserving your capital. Risk has been reduced. You'll be as pleased as a well-tipped waiter when this happens.

3. Wealth creation is accelerated.

With a momentum or trend investing approach, you're able to benefit from rising stock price appreciation over a relatively short period of time compared to the overall stock market. When you side with Mr. Market with a stock that is experiencing a rapid rise in stock price, this fast-paced acceleration gets you closer to reaching your financial objectives. And when you couple covered call options with stock price appreciation, this accelerates the speed at which you're generating wealth even more. You'll be as excited as a donkey with hot pepper up his behind.

This brings us to one of the downsides or challenges of selling covered calls on momentum stocks you own. You run the risk of your stock being called away at any time the current stock price reaches the strike price of your option contract. This means your stock would be sold and the cash would be deposited into your brokerage account.

You still get to keep the option premium and any stock price appreciation gained. However, you run the risk of the stock jumping in price to new levels and missing out on capturing those gains unless you buy back in at a higher valuation. This in itself is not a critical scenario. It just means you'll need to have some option selling criteria in place allowing you to capture both the premiums and stock price appreciation.

This observation brings up the point that you won't be able to realistically sell option contracts every month on momentum stocks you have in play. Your decision to write a contract must take into account both the individual stock's rate of price appreciation as well as the growth rate of the overall market.

Ideally, you want to allow the natural momentum of

the market and stock itself to drive the value upwards without increasing risk or limiting your gains. For example, if the stock is increasing by 4 or 5 percent per month, why risk making only 3 percent with an option's play not knowing how quickly the stock will rise in successive months. Options trading makes more sense when there is a temporary slowdown in stock price appreciation. This is something we'll explore in greater detail coming up.

What do you need to do to sell a call option?

Besides knowing which stock you'll be selling covered calls on, there are four requirements you'll need to meet in order to sell any option contract. These four bits of information you'll need to enter into your online brokerage account are:

1. The expiration date for the contract.
2. The strike price for the option.
3. The number of option contracts.
4. The desired premium price.

All four parameters can be determined or found in the "option chain" for a particular call option. The option chain lists all of the strike prices for the stock for a particular month. Let's start by looking at how long you want to hold onto any option contract.

1. The expiration date for the contract.

Once you log into your online option trading platform and selected the stock you want to trade in the options market, you'll want to choose a contract period. Most option contracts for a particular stock will be listed according to monthly expiration dates.

All option contracts have a limited life expectancy. This is indicated by the contract expiration date. The one-month time period is the most popular time frame used by option's traders like yourself.

The reason why will become obvious. When you sell option contracts on stock you're holding, your primary goal is to generate a premium which will hopefully provide you with a monthly net return of 1 to 3 percent when you factor in transaction costs and the type of option strategy being employed. You also want to decrease the probability your stock will be called away should the stock price rise up to the strike price.

This is best accomplished with monthly contracts. The balance between transaction costs and premium received is best achieved with monthly contracts. Also, the shorter the contract duration the less time the buyer has to see the current stock price rise up to the strike price they would get the stock at.

In contrast, weekly contracts do minimize the time

period, which is an ideal scenario. However, the transaction costs in comparison to the option returns generated may prove to be less profitable. This is one reason why most sellers of covered calls prefer trading on a monthly basis.

A monthly contract also allows the momentum investor a degree of flexibility in adjusting to market momentum swings. Because stock and market volatility are a factor in momentum stock investing, you want to keep your exit strategies simple and manageable.

2. The strike price for the option.

The strike price is the stock price you agree to sell your shares at. For this to happen, the current stock price must rise up to this threshold value. Your stock can then be sold at any time the current stock price reaches the strike price.

In most scenarios, your stock will be sold and your shares assigned to the buyer on the last day of the contract, which is expiration Friday. Most option traders like to wait until the last minute to act upon an option contract. The exception to this unwritten rule is when the stock soars well above the strike price.

Strike prices can be above, at or below the current price of the stock. When selecting a strike price, you'll be looking at those which are above the current stock price. Your primary goal with option plays is to tap into an additional income stream while also benefitting from stock price appreciation.

This is accomplished by ideally selecting a strike price which is out-of-the-money or OTM. A somewhat riskier alternative is to sell an at-the-money ATM option. An ATM call is one in which the current price of the stock is approximately equal to the strike price. ATM premiums being paid are juicier than OTM options.

However, you also risk seeing your stock being called away since the current stock price is at the strike price. This particular approach should really only be used when you would like to exit your stock position for whatever reason. For example, you could sell ATM calls when one of your exit criteria previously discussed in Chapter 6 have been reached.

3. The number of option contracts.

Option contracts are only sold in round lots of 100 shares, which is why I made the case for purchasing your stock in blocks of 100 shares. When starting out with a small amount of capital for your stock purchases, it becomes more challenging to enter the options market and receive a decent return. Here's what I mean.

The transaction costs for options trading for the first contract are normally substantially higher than those for additional contracts. Transaction fees for one option contract will eat away at your option returns more so than four or five contracts. This is why I always recommend selling four or five contracts whenever possible. This seems to be a sweet spot for option plays in balancing transaction costs with expected returns.

Now, I realize you may not have the capital to purchase 400 or 500 shares of stock for any one company, especially if you're allocating your total capital properly across 8 to 10 holdings. In the off-chance Mr. Market looks favourably upon you and presents some hum dinger buying opportunities for 400 or 500 shares of undervalued stock, you might get lucky. If so, head to your favorite watering hole and ask the bartender for an upside-down margarita. You're golden.

In all likelihood, you'll need to weigh the cost of the option transaction against your anticipated returns from the option. When your net monthly option return drops below 1 percent, the amount of risk may outweigh any potential rewards. We'll look at this particular dilemma in detail in a coming chapter.

Now, as previously mentioned, the current price war between online discount brokers has kept transaction costs down. In the case whereby these fees should increase over time, it's best to anticipate the impact on your bottom line. You don't want to be caught with your pants down, do you?

4. The desired premium price.

The most lucrative premiums, from an income generation point of view, are those closest to the actual price of the stock. To entice option traders to invest in these contracts, the reward in doing so has to be balanced with the risk of the stock being called away over the course of the contract. Since the stock can theoretically be called away anytime, an option trader wants to be adequately compensated for the higher risk.

The greater the strike price is from the current stock price the smaller the amount of premium income one can derive from the option. There is less risk of the stock being called away since it has to appreciate in value up to the higher strike price over the course of the option contract. This lower risk equates to a smaller initial premium.

Along with each strike price, you'll see the current "ask" and "bid" prices for the premiums. The asking price is what the sellers for a particular option contract are wanting. The asking price is always more than the bid price. The bidding price is what the buyers are willing to pay for that contract. This value is always lower than the asking price.

So, what does all this mean? The bid price is what you can expect Mr. Market to pay for your option contracts. This means you should use this lower value as your initial gauge in determining how much of an option premium you might receive when you sell your option contracts.

The converse is true. Should you want to buy back your option contracts, the ask price is the value you should base your initial expectations on. Buying back your option contracts will cost you more money than to sell them and receive a premium.

As you can see, option contracts have a spread between the bid and ask prices. When you place your orders in the options market, you'll want to take this into consideration. The narrower the spread the easier it is to create profitable outcomes in the options market. Well-established companies with large market caps in excess of $250 million and moderate to low stock price volatility tend to have narrower spreads.

Use the same approach to selling (or buying) your option contracts as you used for purchasing your initial shares of stock. You have a choice between selling your shares with a "market" order or a "limit" order.

By selecting "market order" in your online option trading platform, you're expecting the order to be filled at the current bid price for that option. Doing so, ensures you get filled quickly. At least faster than most limit orders.

Entering a limit order on your option trading platform, requires you wait to see if a buyer on the other end of the trade will accept your limit order. The options market is very dynamic with option contracts being sold and bought normally within a narrow trading range.

If you're patient and willing to wait for developments to unfold, you can often obtain a slightly better premium by placing a limit order. One effective strategy is to place a limit order between the lower bid price and the mid-price for the option. The mid-price is the price of an option contract half-way between the bid and ask prices. This means you'll be placing a limit order which is slightly higher than what you would expect for a market order.

I'll often place my limit orders this way. I typically wait an hour or two to see if a buyer has taken me up on the offer. When they do, I gleefully rub my hands like a 5-year old in an ice-cream parlor. If not, I'll either wait a bit longer before the markets close or adjust my limit order slightly.

Now that you have a better idea as to what options contracts can do for your stock portfolio and what key parameters you need to take into consideration, let's explore how to best enter the options market in the following chapter.

8

ENTERING THE OPTIONS MARKET

You're about to explore those parameters you need to have in place for entering the options market. The guidelines outlined below will increase your chances of coming out on top. To enter the market, you'll be following the process of "selling to open" an option contract. But before we look at the specifics, it may be helpful to start our discussion with a quick look at how you should set things up.

What should you take into consideration when selecting a broker?

With a momentum trading approach, coupled with the occasional options trade, the number of potential transactions increases. Therefore, being cognizant of the number of transactions and associated fees is an important portfolio management skill. With small capital allocations across several momentum stocks, you want to focus on reducing costs as much as feasible. This can be accomplished in part by using the services of an online discount broker.

Some of the factors to consider when selecting a particular online discount broker are:

- Account minimums.
- The fee structure for buying and selling equities.
- The fee structure for buying and selling option contracts.
- Access to paper trading simulations.
- The extent of technical charting tools available.
- Access to in-depth and comprehensive investment reports.
- Ease in navigating the site.
- The level of customer service available.
- Access to free stock and option investing educational resources.

A simple way of assessing these criteria is to Google the term "online discount brokers compared". You can then get a feel for some of the top discount brokers on these comparative sites. Just be careful the comparative site you're exploring is not playing specific favourites for one particular online platform over all the others.

The best type of account to consider setting up within your brokerage's platform is one allowing you to generate wealth tax-free. This can be accomplished with a Roth IRA account (TFSA in Canada). A Roth IRA allows you to deposit income that has already been taxed into the account where any returns are able to compound tax-free. These tax-free gains can then be withdrawn as you see fit such as funding a college education, paying for a family vacation or going towards purchasing your dream home.

Once you have your account set up with your online discount broker, it's time to learn before you earn. Getting a feel for stock and option investing takes a bit of time to get used to. This is why most experienced stock investors recommend starting out by paper trading for several months, especially with options trading.

With a momentum trading approach to stock investing, you'll be trying to capitalize on the rapid price appreciation of a particular stock. Whenever the stock market experiences a major setback, you often have many months of potential uphill growth before the momentum slows down.

During this period of time, you have an opportune

time to learn before you earn in the options market. This can be accomplished through paper trading. Some discount brokers have simulation platforms set up whereby you can buy and sell equities and options using paper money, not unlike in the games of Monopoly or CashFlow.

Paper trading makes a lot of sense when you're waiting for a slowdown in momentum growth for your particular stock holdings. It's at this point in time you'll look to potential option plays to bolster your overall returns. In the meantime, make use of this downtime to educate yourself as to the ins and outs of options trading.

Which brings us to look at what specific information you need to take into account, so as to increase your probability of a positive outcome in the options market.

What key selection criteria increase option trading success?

When choosing between two relatively equal momentum plays, always lean towards the stock which is also being actively traded in the options market. This enables you to generate an additional income stream from writing covered calls. It also creates downside protection for your stock price, since a cash premium is being deposited into your brokerage account. This cash injection lowers your cost basis for the stock reducing your risk level.

As for some of the specific criteria to investigate with each options trade consider the following:

1. Market cap of the stock.

The market cap or capitalization reflects the size of the company you're dealing with. Market cap is calculated by multiplying the stock's current price by the total number of outstanding shares in the market. Outstanding shares are all those shares held by investors and company officers.

A rule of thumb I follow in determining if a company is large enough for me to trade options with a degree of confidence is seeing a market cap of at least $250 million. You may wish to only look at businesses with a market cap in excess of $500 million to build in some degree of assurance the company is large enough to safely move into and out of option positions. The smaller the company, the higher the potential volatility in the markets.

2. Current range of option premiums.

The sweet spot for most conservative monthly covered call traders is being able to generate an option return of 1 to 4 percent.

At the upper end a 4 percent return would be for an at-the-money call ATM, which provides the highest returns but also carries with it a high probability of your stock being called away. Recall, that premiums are the juiciest when the current stock price is equal to the strike price. For increased risk of being exercised, option traders expect more of a reward in option premiums to compensate for the risk.

A 1 percent return would be best reflected in the premium being generated for an out-of-the-money OTM call. The further the strike price is above the current stock price the lower the option return. A 1 to 2 percent return for an OTM call close to the current stock price is a reasonable expectation and goal to aspire to attain.

3. Bid-ask spread and open interest.

The narrower the spread between the bidding price and the asking price for an option contract, the better for entering and exiting option positions. A narrow spread means you'll spend less to close any position.

Often, a wide bid-ask spread is a reflection of the number of option contracts being actively traded in the market. With fewer option contracts being traded, you may not be able to exit the options market when you would like to and at a price that keeps you in positive territory.

Also, you want to see a certain volume of interest in option trades occurring. For each seller of an options contract there must be a buyer. Until a contact has been sold and bought, thus closing the transaction, it is considered to be open. Looking at the open interest ensures there is enough trading volume occurring to safely move into and out of a position.

As a rule of thumb, only consider those options contracts having an at-the-money ATM bid-ask spread less than 30 cents with an ATM opening interest greater than 100.

4. Option volatility.

When option returns rise above 4 percent, premiums generated can be quite lucrative. Unfortunately, with higher returns comes increased option volatility, which also means higher stock price volatility.

True, volatility is our friend in the stock market. It can present some interesting stock and option plays. However, excessive volatility comes with increased risk of loss either through stock or option positions moving in the opposite direction than desired or anticipated. You may be forced to exit positions prematurely when wide swings occur in the stock's price.

As a side note, when you do see a particular momentum stock plateauing in upward price movement and you decide to capture an option premium for this lull in the stock's movement, you'll need to remove your automatic stop-loss stock order and manually monitor any price declines. Recall that you were encouraged to use a 15 percent stop-loss limit for your stock holdings as an exit strategy to protect you from excessive capital loss.

Depending on your online discount broker and the type of options trading account you have set up, your broker may not allow you to exit your stock position with a stop loss when you have a covered call. By being allowed to exit your stock position with the sale of your holding, you've now moved from a covered to a "naked" position. Some options accounts limit your ability to trade naked calls. Check with your broker beforehand to see what rules they'll be abiding by.

5. Shares traded per day.

Finally, a fourth consideration is looking at the volume of transactions occurring in the stock market to gauge if there is enough activity and interest in your particular stock. You want to see investors actively trading the stock in question. If investors are sidelined and few shares are being traded, you may be hard-pressed to sell (and buy back) your option contracts, if need be.

A simple rule of thumb to follow is to only consider

those stocks having a trade volume of at least 250,000 shares per day.

What these four criteria do is ensure there is enough interest to be able to move into and out of option positions with minimal costs. As in selecting momentum stocks, we want to see the same pattern of interest by Mr. Market when considering option plays.

What type of order should you place?

When you log into your online brokerage account, you'll have a choice between trading stocks and trading options for a particular stock. When you select one of your momentum stocks and you would like to explore selling option contracts as upward momentum slows, you'll want to check out the options trading platform in your brokerage account.

Clicking on the link to the options trading platform from within your online brokerage account and selecting the stock in question, takes you to the option chain for that particular stock. Once there, you'll see a number of option months listed. Clicking on the most recent month will pull up at a minimum a list of strike prices and their corresponding bid and ask prices. You'll also probably see information related to the open interest, volume and the price of the last transaction settled.

Often both calls and puts are displayed on your screen. You should be able to deselect the puts being displayed with a simple click of a toggle. We're most interested in call options.

After some investigating of those strike prices closest to the current price of the stock, you'll be placing a "sell to open" limit order when you're ready to sell your option contracts. This limit order should initially be set between the lower bid price and the mid-price for the contract. The approach is the same one suggested earlier for purchasing shares of stock.

Selecting which strike price to use will be based on the strategy being used and the overall growth potential offered. We'll look at how to arrive at which strike price to select in the next chapter. Ready to get started? I know some of you were ready yesterday.

9

THE ONLY TWO OPTION STRATEGIES TO FOCUS ON.

FOR THE CONSERVATIVE covered call writer, you have a handful of tried and true option strategies in your arsenal available to you. For the purposes of this guide, you'll be most interested in those strategies capturing both the upside momentum of stock price appreciation along with some monthly income generation through option premiums.

The two strategies you'll be using are:

1. The growth generation strategy.
2. The income generation strategy.

The growth generation strategy takes advantage of stock price appreciation along with some monthly income production. The other looks more at income production with no or little upside stock price appreciation.

Once you understand how these strategies work, we'll look at some case studies to put everything into perspective in Chapter 10. In fact, you really only need one such strategy to focus your attention on and that is the growth strategy.

The Growth Generation Strategy:

A growth strategy is based on the premise of using an out-of-the-money OTM call. Before discussing the ideal conditions of using a growth play and how to set it up, let's touch on the advantages and disadvantages of using this strategy with momentum stocks.

There are three main advantages of using a growth strategy in conjunction with your momentum plays:

- Since you'll be using OTM calls, you benefit from the option premium received, as well as any stock price appreciation up to the strike price. Even if your stock is called away, you pocket both a cash premium and the new stock value at the strike price.
- The chances for your stock being called away and sold on you should the current stock price rise up to the strike price are reduced. A higher strike price means more upward stock

price movement over the course of a month in order for the stock to be exercised.

- Time decay works in your favor. By selecting a 1-month period of time, the stock has a limited window of opportunity to rise up to the strike price. Also, as time expires, the value of the option premium approaches zero, which means it takes less cash to buy back and close your open position if need be.

Unfortunately, there are also three main disadvantages you'll need to weigh into the decision-making matrix before trading options with the growth strategy. The key disadvantages to take into consideration are:

- Amongst all of the option trading strategies, this one produces the least amount of downside protection should the stock price decline.
- This strategy generates the lowest initial option premium. This is because the further away the strike price is from the current price, the lower the risk and premiums received.
- Unfortunately, when the stock price drops significantly and you want to exit your stock position, it'll cost you more to close your option position.

Any conservative option trading strategy should not be used with rapidly rising stocks or markets. It's much smarter to capture the natural momentum of the stock with stock price appreciation on its own. No need to risk losing out on rapid growth by trying to force greater returns with a covered call strategy.

A simple rule of thumb to use for assessing whether or not you should entertain the notion of using a growth strategy is by comparing the stock price appreciation with the option return generated. If your stock price is growing over 4 percent per month, sit on the sidelines with option plays. No need to take on any unnecessary risk.

As you know, the stock market and stock price appreciation for a particular stock rarely rise up in a linear fashion. It bounces up and down. Healthy markets move in a wave-like pattern rising and falling while on an upward trajectory. The growth generation strategy works best when stock growth has temporarily stalled, and you would like to generate capital growth over a short 1-month period of time.

How do you put the growth strategy into play?

You've already looked at four technical indicators used in conjunction with stock charts to assess momentum stocks. These same indicators will be used to determine if an option growth play is unfolding for one of your holdings.

There are four parameters you want to see when implementing the growth strategy. When these conditions unfold, it makes the options trade more conducive to using a growth strategy. These four conditions are:

1. Steady upward stock price and market movement.
2. 50-day moving average moving in a positive direction.
3. Relative Strength Index above 50 but below 80.
4. Moving Average Convergence Divergence indicating a positive trend.

Let's look at each of these parameters in greater detail.

1. Steady upward stock and market movement.

With any growth strategy, you want to see the technical charts moving upwards in a positive direction with minimal price movement swings or excessive volatility in the markets. Take a look at both the stock's price and trading volume over the last few months. What you would like to see is the graphic for the daily price of the stock rising steadily on average to above average volume.

Also, take a look at a technical chart of a broad-based index like the S&P 500 to get a feel for the overall market sentiments. You're looking for positive growth over several months of trading, indicating that we're in a bull market or positive trend.

2. 50-day moving average moving in a positive direction.

When looking at the 50-day MA for your stock, ensure it is continuing to rise above the 200-day MA. You want to confirm the stock price is moving in a positive direction. As well, look at the volume to see if it's rising along with the stock price. Positive momentum shows up when both volume and stock prices are rising. Trading volume is a good indicator as to whether or not investors are putting their money on the line for purchasing shares of stock.

The volume should also be steadily rising. Sharp changes in volume often indicate increased volatility and potential stock price corrections about to happen or in the process of unfolding.

3. Relative Strength Index above 50 but below 80.

Recall that the RSI is a technical chart momentum indicator displayed as a line graph moving between two extremes zero and 100. It measures the magnitude of recent price changes and can be used to assess if your stock is currently overbought or oversold.

You want to see this momentum indicator in positive territory for a growth generation options play. However, avoid popping into the options market when this metric rises above 80. High RSI values indicate the stock is moving into overbought territory and large institutional traders may begin to unload the stock soon. It's best to wait for all of the stars to line up before committing. Otherwise, you may find it as challenging as pushing a wet noodle up a hill in trying to generate a return.

4. Moving Average Convergence Divergence indicating a positive trend.

When looking at a histogram or bar chart of the MACD for your stock, determine if the trend is moving above the zero line into positive territory or not. This indicator uses two moving averages of stock price for helping to assess the direction of a trend. An upward momentum trend is indicated by a bar chart which is heading upwards above the zero line.

Once you've assessed if these four technical indicators are driving stock price momentum upwards, you can now look at specific option plays. Your goal is to analyze a couple of call options to see what sort of returns you could generate with an options play.

The easiest approach to follow is to use an options profit calculator. There are many free versions available online. And one of the best online calculators is the Ellman Calculator, which can be downloaded for free from The Blue Collar Investor website. This calculator does a lot of the heavy lifting when churning out the numbers.

An alternative to using one of these online tools is to create a scaled down version using an electronic spreadsheet that'll calculate your option return and total return when you plug in your numbers.

First of all, you'll want to log into your online brokerage platform, select the stock in question and look at the options chain for that equity. Once you're on your options trading platform look for the current month's option chain. It will list all of the strike prices for the month.

Next, using your calculator, you'll need to enter four pieces of data for each option contract being analyzed onto your spreadsheet, as follows:

1. The strike price of the two options above the current price of the stock.
2. The bid price (or lower value) of each of the two options.
3. The price you paid for the stock.

4. The number of option contracts you'd like to sell.

Your option calculator will provide you with a quick snapshot of what your option and total returns could be. These calculations indicate what your hypothetical maximum returns would be. They take into account how much cash you would receive if your stock was called away at the selected strike price.

Deciding on which strike price to go with will depend on:

- How much premium you'll receive up front versus what the stock price appreciation potential might be.
- How profitable the transaction will be when both the options premium and stock price appreciation potential up to the strike price are taken into account.

As previously mentioned, option returns of less than 1 percent may not make sense financially. You'll want to compare the transaction fees being charged in relation to the return you'll generate. If no significant financial gain can be realized don't risk writing a contract.

Option returns of 1 to 2 percent can prove to be profitable, depending on the numbers of contracts

SCOTT DOUGLAS

being sold. Remember, option contracts are sold in round lots of 100 shares. More often than not, option plays with 4 or 5 contracts tend to produce acceptable return levels, when you factor in fees.

However, online discount broker fees dropped significantly in late 2019. As long as the discount brokers duke it out, you'll benefit from the lower cost of doing business.

Option returns of 2 to 3 percent are entering our sweet zone for monthly returns. Option returns for the growth generation strategy above 3 percent may prove to be too volatile. Should you be wanting to hold onto the stock for its upside potential, wide stock price swings may test your patience.

As for your overall returns generated, you'll want to know how profitable your options play will be when you look at the maximum hypothetical return that could be generated. This is calculated by adding your option premium received to the value of your stock at the strike price.

Ask yourself: Is this combined return potentially greater than just the anticipated return of the stock appreciating in value without doing an options play?

If the combined return offers a significant advantage in growth potential, then this option trade may prove to be lucrative. However, if there is no material change in the anticipated growth by entering the options market, you're best served by not exposing yourself to any increased risk. Can you imagine how much frustration this could save you?

The Income Generation Strategy:

The income generation strategy attempts to capture the highest option premiums available for a particular month. This strategy should be used sparingly with momentum stocks. It's really only useful when momentum has slowed to a standstill and you may have to exit your stock position soon. In other words, stock price appreciation may have slowed to a trickle and momentum is shifting.

To execute this option strategy, you'll only focus on selling an at-the-money call with the expectation you'll have your stock called away by month's end. When you sell ATM calls with a strike price mirroring the current price of the stock, there is a higher probability the stock will remain at or above the current price and be exercised.

You benefit by:

- Profiting from the highest initial option returns. Premiums tend to be the richest.
- Generating cash flow despite no or little stock

price appreciation. Great if you're planning on exiting your stock position anyway.

On the downside:

- You won't benefit from any stock price appreciation over the course of the month since the calls are at-the-money.
- You have a high probability of being called away. This strategy should not be used with stocks you want to hold onto long-term.

How do you put the income strategy into play?

As with the growth strategy, there are four parameters you want to see when implementing the income strategy. These four conditions are:

1. No appreciable stock price and market movement is occurring.
2. 50-day and 200-day moving averages are converging.
3. Relative Strength Index is oscillating between 30 and 80.
4. Moving Average Convergence Divergence is relatively flat.

Let's explore these in greater detail.

1. No appreciable stock price and market movement.

When graphs of the stock market and your stock are flattening out, it can indicate the end of a momentum trend, especially on average volume. A drop in transaction volume coupled with sideways trading is a sure sign the tide is about to shift.

2. 50-day and 200-day moving averages are converging.

When these two averages begin to flatten out, the stock is showing signs of losing upward momentum. The growth trend may soon end. Time to consider an exit strategy with an options play.

3. Relative Strength Index oscillating between 30 and 80.

A rising RSI from 50 to 80 usually indicates buyers are pumping money into the stock. When the RSI is not showing any clear direction signals, it may indicate that a momentum trend is ending.

4. Moving Average Convergence Divergence being relatively flat.

When the MACD is not giving any clear signals as to the direction of the momentum and the histogram is relatively flat, this often indicates momentum is shifting.

The appearance of these four conditions is a sure sign positive upward momentum is shifting and you should explore using an income generation strategy to hopefully capture some gains before possibly exiting your position.

As with the growth generation strategy, you'll need to enter four pieces of data for the option contract being analyzed onto your spreadsheet, as follows:

1. The strike price closest to the current price of the stock.
2. The bid price or premium being paid for that option.
3. The price you paid for the stock.
4. The number of option contracts you'd like to sell.

With the income generation strategy, you want to capture the highest premiums possible. Monthly option premiums in the range of 2 to 4 percent are common.

You also have to accept the notion your stock will likely be called away. Not a bad deal, if you were planning on selling your holding anyways.

In the next chapter, you'll find out how to exit your option positions safely. This is much easier to accomplish when compared to trying to comb your hair with a push broom.

10

EXITING THE OPTIONS MARKET

As YOU KNOW NOW, when you write covered calls the transaction you initiate is a sell-to-open order. You're starting your option order by selling contracts on stock you own. When you need to close your position, you'll enter a "buy-to close" order for your covered calls. This is the exact opposite process to writing your initial contracts.

The primary objective of using covered calls is to generate an additional monthly stream of income. In an ideal situation, you would:

- Sell an option contract on stock you own.
- Benefit immediately from a cash premium.
- Generate an option return of 1 to 4 percent.

- Allow the option contract to expire worthless, to your advantage.

However, not all transactions go as planned. You must also have a repertoire of exit strategies to fall back on when situations don't work out as planned. Some situations can cost you money, others are opportunities to generate additional cash.

When do you use option exit strategies?

You should consider exiting any covered call position when one of the following four conditions crops up:

1. Your stock is in danger.
2. You can pick up an 80 percent option premium gain within the first 2 weeks.
3. You can pick up a 90 percent gain in week 3.
4. Your stock is at the strike price in week 4.

Time to explore each of these scenarios in greater detail.

1. Your stock is in danger.

When your momentum stock triggers one of the safeguards in place for exiting any position, you need to heed the warning and exit your positions. Should the current stock price drop 15 percent from your initial purchase price, or the 50-day and 200-day moving averages cross over from positive to negative territory, it's time to close your positions.

You'll need to close your option positions first, before selling the stock. To do so, place a buy-to-close order for your option contracts being held. This is the exact opposite of your sell-to-open order. This means you'll need to have a small cash reserve in your brokerage account in order to pay for closing your positions. A cash reserve of 5 percent of your stock holdings is often recommended for just this scenario. If you've received 2 or 3 percent when selling your contracts, expect to incur slightly higher costs to close your positions.

You can enter either a market or limit order, depending on your level of comfort in closing your positions and the expediency of having to exit your positions. A market order will be executed the fastest, giving you a little more peace of mind. The downside is you could end up paying a little more for closing your position.

To place a limit order, enter a bid which is between the mid-price and asking price for your option. The asking price is the higher value displayed in the option chain between the bid and ask prices. You may need to be patient over the course of several hours for Mr. Market to find an appropriate seller who'll take your money. Use this approach if you're confident you can close your positions with a significant saving and urgency is not a factor.

Once your option contracts are closed, you're free to sell your stock holdings. Again, you can enter either a market or limit order for the transaction. Should you decide to use a limit order, place this order slightly above the current price in the markets.

Personally, I like to enter market orders when I need to exit my positions quickly. I'm already thinking of the next opportunity around the corner. This means I've emotionally taken myself out of the exit equation. I don't become emotionally attached to any particular holding.

2. You can pick up an 80 percent option premium gain within the first 2 weeks.

The opposite of having to exit your positions because of negative changes in the stock, is taking money off the table and profiting from your option contracts. This scenario pans out when you have a monthly option contract with a 4-week time span. If you had a 5-week time span, the 80 percent rule applies to the first 3 weeks.

When the price of your option drops to less than 20 percent of what you received in premiums, buy back the contract. You've now received a substantial gain within a short period of time. This gain materializes because the stock price is dropping. As the stock price drops so does the value of the current option premium. It now becomes less expensive to close your position. By closing your option position, you're free to enter the option market again should the stock price rise and a favourable premium be generated.

3. You can pick up a 90 percent gain in week 3.

As in the above scenario, when the current option premium is less than 10 percent of what you received it's time to cash in. As time to option contract expiration diminishes, expect to capture a higher percentage of the premium available to make it worthwhile. With less time for an option play to unfold, plan on being rewarded more for your efforts. And as above, if you're in a 5-week month, look at buying back your option contracts up to the end of week 4. In either case, you want to capture your option premiums and be in the position to re-enter the option market when opportunity knocks.

4. Your stock is at the strike price in week 4.

It's not uncommon for a momentum stock to appreciate in value up to the strike price you've set in your initial option contract. You should be giddy when this happens as you've probably benefited from both stock price appreciation and capturing an option premium. Wouldn't it be skookum if you could rinse and repeat this outcome?

You have a couple of choices at month end. The first is just allowing the stock to be called away on expiration Friday. By next Monday morning you'll have cash from the sale of your stock at the strike price plus any option premiums deposited at the beginning of the month.

The second choice is to plan on holding onto your stock and selling another option contract for the following month. In this case, you'll need to close your current option position and then sell an option contract for the next month. You maintain control over your momentum stock position and can ride it up to higher returns. Which brings the conversation around to discuss ...

What two exit strategies do you need to know?

Both of the exit strategies discussed below involve rolling your current option position from one month to the next. These rolling strategies work best when your momentum stock has appreciated up to or even past the strike price you sold your initial option contracts at.

They can be used anytime in the last week of the option cycle but are most often initiated on expiration Friday when option premiums are lowest. Doing so on expiration Friday makes sense since the cost of buying back your current option contracts to close them out is lower. Here's how each strategy plays out.

1. Rolling forward and up.

Use this particular rolling strategy into the next month when your stock price has appreciated up past the strike price you initially selected, and you would like to hang onto the stock. The market signals to keep an eye on that are favourable for this strategy are:

- Positive upward movement of the stock market as a whole.
- Continuing strong stock growth and solid financial fundamentals.
- Technical indicators showing continued positive signs of growth.

Here are the three steps to follow for rolling out and up:

1. Close your current option contracts by buying back the contracts.
2. Select the strike price just above the current stock price for the next month.
3. Enter a sell-to-open order to capture the next month's premium.

Closing your current position will cost you some money. However, selling the next month's higher strike should offset the closing costs. The net effect should be having maintained control over your momentum stock and profiting from an injection of cash for the sale of your new option contract.

When you buy back your contracts, you're in effect buying back the equity in the stock since it has appreciated in value over the course of the month. By doing nothing and allowing your stock to be called away, you lose out on the opportunity to generate an additional monthly return from your options.

This option strategy takes advantage of you benefitting from stock price appreciation along with a little bit of monthly option income.

2. Rolling forward.

The rolling forward strategy is best used when:

- The overall market tone is giving mixed signals.
- The stock's fundamentals are still showing signs of growth.
- The stock's technicals are beginning to show mixed signs that momentum is slowing.

Despite your momentum stock showing favourable

signs of company growth in the fundamentals department, Mr. Market may not always concur. A technical chart of the stock and market as a whole may be indicating that your stock is falling out of favour with investors. The momentum trend for stock price appreciation may be coming to an end.

Use the rolling forward strategy to capture some upside growth potential remaining. You may wish to employ this strategy knowing that in all likelihood the probability of your stock being called away increases with this approach.

To roll out, you'll want to follow these three steps:

1. Close out your current option position by buying back your contract.
2. Select the strike price closest to the current stock price for the next month.
3. Place your sell-to-open option order to lock in next month's premium.

You're attempting to benefit from the maximum amount of premium available for the new option contract you'll be selling. Of course, this is with the understanding your stock has a high probability of being called away over the next month.

This scenario can work towards your advantage, if

you're planning on exiting your momentum stock soon. It also can be beneficial if the markets are fluctuating and at month's end your stock has not moved. In this case, you could wait for the option contract to expire worthless, then sell another contract for the following month. Even if your stock price appreciation stalls you can still continue to earn monthly call premiums. A pretty sweet deal.

All of this theory gives you some insights into what you could be doing. However, it won't become crystal clear until you see some actual examples. In the following chapter, you'll experience first-hand various case studies incorporating all of the notions presented so far in your guide. This should provide you with a deeper level of understanding as to how you could structure your momentum plays. Ready for some inspiration?

STOCK MARKET REBOUND CASE STUDIES

IT'S NOW time to look at putting all this sage advice into practice by walking through a few case studies. By experiencing firsthand how various situations could play out, you'll be in a better position to make the right decisions for your own momentum trades. Seeing is believing. And what better way to convey the basic concepts than by looking at specific examples. Ready to get started?

In all of these case studies, we're going to make some basic assumptions to simplify the math and concepts being covered. Thanks to a pricing war in the fall of 2019, many regular stock trades are now $0. These fees were previously averaging $7 to $10 per transaction. We're going to assume the pricing war is going to continue throughout 2020 and into 2021 as the economy rebounds from the coronavirus pandemic.

For options trades many discount brokers are offering a base rate for entering the options market of $0 with a $.75 commission charge per contract. So, if you were to sell 3 contracts, it would cost you $2.25. Previously the fees for entering the options market were averaging between $7 and $10, along with a commission of approximately $1 per contract. Given this context, you could expect to disperse up to $13 in total fees for selling or buying 3 option contracts. As above, we'll assume the option transaction fees are at a minimum for right now.

The first hypothetical scenario to look at is comparing a momentum stock purchase of just 100 shares of stock with one involving 300. This'll enable you to better grasp the upside potential of using options trading in conjunction with a momentum play. It'll also illustrate how transaction fees come into play when assessing profitability.

Case Study #1: Small Position with a Momentum Stock

In the first situation, let's assume you would like to invest up to $1500 in the Popeye Spinach Company (POP), which is currently trading at $15 per share. The stock has dropped from its recent 52-week high of $60 and is currently trading at a bargain. Given the current share price, you would be able to pick up 100 shares of stock.

The company has had consistent growth in sales of 16 percent over the past several years. It seems that there has been a national surge in the popularity of green drink smoothies and spinach omelettes driving revenues for the company. Along with solid sales growth, both the return on invested capital and earnings per share growth rates are in double digit territory. It seems management is doing a very good job managing its capital investments and shareholders are being rewarded.

Not only are the financials showing promise, but Mr. Market has embraced the stock, which has seen significant stock price appreciation over the past three months with above average volume. Institutional buyers are on board with investing in this market leader within the food industry.

The 50-day moving average has remained above the 200-day moving average for months now, showing no signs of letting up. The Relative Strength Index is high, oscillating between 70 and 80. Yet, this is still within our potential buy parameters. The most recent weekly trend in momentum shows the Moving Average

Convergence Divergence indicator in positive momentum territory.

All of the signals, both fundamental and technical, are lining up indicating a buy signal. You decide to jump right in and pick up 100 shares. At the same time, you set a stop loss order for your holding at $12.75, which represents a 15 percent drop in the stock's price. Should Popeye Spinach drop below this threshold your holding would be cashed out preventing any further potential loss.

Over the next month, Popeye Spinach's share price climbs at a steady rate of 3 to 4 percent. You're wondering if you should sell 1 out-of-the-money contract of POP in the options market to increase your cash flow into your brokerage account.

Given the cost of 1 contract is less than $1, this seems like a good opportunity. However, we need to look at the current price movement of the stock in comparison to the option premium received to judge whether the risk is worth it.

The first step is to determine what dollar value a 3 to 4 percent price appreciation is currently providing you for your holding. On the low end, 3 percent of a $1500 investment generates a monthly return of approximately $45. And on the high end a 4 percent return produces roughly $60 in the first month or so of holding onto Popeye Spinach.

Contrast this with entering the options market. Let's assume a current stock price of $15.50 with an out-of-the-money call having a strike price (16) expiring in one month has a premium of 15 cents. Recall, strike prices closest to the current price produce the sweetest option returns. In this case an OTM covered call generates a lower option return. A 15-cent premium with a $15.50 stock price equates to less than 1 percent in option premiums.

However, this isn't the entire picture. True your option return creates a return which is less than 1 percent. But, when you take into account stock price appreciation up to the strike price, this produces a theoretical maximum return of roughly 4 percent.

You would hypothetically receive 50 cents per share from the price appreciation of Popeye Spinach up from the current price of $15.50 to $16, along with the initial 15 cents per share deposited into your brokerage account for initiating the covered call. When you subtract the low commission rate of 75 cents for the total transaction, this means you would potentially receive a maximum of $64.25.

Now, comes the time to analyze the profitability of each situation while factoring in the risk. We're going to compare the recent growth potential of moving from $15.50 up to $16 and not the overall growth from the initial purchase price of $15. This is because you're looking at option premium values based on current stock prices.

In the first situation where you just held onto the stock, you only benefit from $50 of stock price appreciation of going from $15.50 to $16 per share (100 shares x $0.50).

Layering on a covered call generates a maximum of $64.25 in total returns ($50 for the maximum stock price appreciation available plus $14.25 in net option premiums). Opting for the options play appears to be the winning strategy as it could generate a higher overall return. But not so fast, my little Jack Russell.

You also have to factor in the risk involved. With transaction fees currently being so low as to be an insignificant factor in the overall returns, you have a distinct advantage in using options plays even with a small holding of 100 shares. But these price war conditions may or may not continue past 2021.

In comparison, under pre-2020 option trading conditions, you paid higher transaction fees. These higher costs would have had an impact on your bottom line. For example, if you were to pay $10 for initiating the option transaction and $1 per contract, you would pay a total of $11 instead of 75 cents for this option play. Now, if you're paid $15 in total premiums, your net profit from the sale of your contract would give you a whopping $4. A far cry from the $14.25 generated when transaction fees are almost non-existent.

Holding onto just the stock, hypothetically generates $50 through stock price appreciation. Selling a covered call would hypothetically give you $54 for the month when higher transaction fees come into the mix. So, option trading with small positions is challenging when trying to remain profitable especially when fees rise.

Another risk factor to assess is what could transpire should your stock be called away. Sure, you max out your total returns, which are higher than just riding up the stock price. Unfortunately, your shares of Popeye Spinach will be exercised at month's end with the cash from the sale being deposited into your brokerage account. Now, you'll need to assess if Popeye Spinach is worthwhile to re-invest in.

If the stock should suddenly jump in price after expiration Friday, you'll pay more to re-enter the position at the higher stock purchase price. Fortunately, this higher re-entry price point is mitigated by the low or non-existent transaction fees currently being assessed. On the flip side, if transaction fees for re-entering the stock market become a consideration in the future, using an option play may prove to be less profitable than just holding onto the stock.

Fortunately, should Popeye Spinach not rise up to the strike price, you won't be exercised, and your total theoretical returns will be slightly less as a result. You won't benefit from the maximum profit potential being generated by using both stock price appreciation and income from premiums being paid to you. However, you do capture an option premium which helps to increase your overall portfolio growth and you're also free to enter another option play if the cards align once again.

So, what can we learn from this particular case study? First, if transaction fees continue to remain low, it's possible for the little guy with just 100 shares of stock to use options trading as a means of creating some additional revenue when risk is factored in.

And second, when deciding between two possible outcomes, select the one with the lower risk potential in lieu of one generating a higher return. A bird in the hand is better than two in the bush. For this particular case study, estimated returns for holding onto just the stock were around 3 to 4 percent. Factoring in an options play raised the potential overall returns slightly above 4 percent. It's not worth taking the risk.

We've just looked at a case in which you only control 100 shares of stock with a small position. What about if you were to hold a bigger position? How would that impact your overall returns and decision-making?

Case Study #2: Larger Position with a Momentum Stock

In our second case study situation, let's assume you have $4500 to invest, which means you would be able to pick up 300 shares of Popeye Spinach. Given the same context and conditions, let's see how things could work out. You pick up 300 shares of POP at $15 per share with no transaction fees being assessed. This initial transaction would cost you $4500.

As before, Popeye Spinach's share price climbs at a steady rate of 3 to 4 percent. A 3 percent growth rate on a $4500 investment represents a hypothetical monthly gain of approximately $135 each month. And a 4 percent stock price appreciation produces about $180 over the course of the first month.

Let's say Popeye Spinach rises in price from your initial buy-in at $15 to $15.50, as before. If we use this as our current stock price and we sell an out-of-the-money call for 15 cents having a strike price of (16) which expires in one month, we would generate an option premium of $45. This amount, less the $2.25 option commission, would be deposited immediately into your brokerage account. Your total potential return, layering on an option play, would generate $192.75 ($150 from stock price appreciation from $15.50 to $16 plus $42.75 in net option returns).

When you contrast this overall maximum growth potential of $192.75 for the month to just stock price appreciation of $150, you can see the upside potential offered by using an option growth strategy. Controlling several option contracts potentially creates a significant overall return, which is much higher than counting on stock price appreciation alone in this particular scenario.

But, what about if you have to pay significantly higher transaction costs. Assuming it'll cost you a $10 base fee for every option transaction and $1 for each contract sold, you could expect to pay $13 when you sell your 3 option contracts. These higher fees reduce your overall maximum growth potential from $192.75 down to $182. Compared to just a stock appreciation potential of $150, you still come out significantly ahead for the month.

So, what sage advice can we gleam from this case study? First, even with higher overall option trading fees, the more contracts you control the greater the profitability potential for your portfolio.

Second, the risk assessment is virtually the same for both case studies. However, because overall transaction fees are lower with more shares under your control, a shift in the risk-reward assessment moves in favour of a more favourable reward outcome.

So, when are the most opportune times to use option plays? Let's take a closer look at one in particular that focuses on when you would like to exit your stock holding.

Case Study #3: Using Covered Calls to Exit a Momentum Play

Whether you're exiting a momentum play because you've captured a 300 percent gain or the stock no longer is panning out, using a one-time options play should be on your mind as an exit strategy. Why not try to capture as much upside potential as possible and exit in a blaze of glory?

To do so you'll need to assess the viability of such an action plan. Here's an example of what could transpire with the Willie Wonka Corporation (WONK). Let's assume you're holding 100 shares of Willie Wonka stock you purchased at an initial stock price of $20 over a year ago.

You felt Willie Wonka had great growth potential with the new release of their online sales platform and quick delivery system. The stock soared to $60 over the span of a year. Then, sales slowed as new competitors entered the online market. The stock retraced some of its gains, settling in at $55 per share, where it has been trading sideways for the past couple of months. With a 275 percent "paper gain", you're wondering if you should exit your position and capture whatever gains you've benefitted from.

A closer examination of the stock shows that revenue sales growth has declined from an initial 18 percent to just under 10 percent. And the other fundamentals are showing signs of wavering as well. Looking at a technical chart of the stock, Mr. Market tends to concur. The 50-day and 200-day moving averages are converging and both the RSI and MACD are showing mixed signs momentum growth is slowing and could reverse.

It's time to exit your position. But how could you capture some additional gains rather than just sell your position outright? The answer my dear friend is by selling an at-the-money covered call.

By selling an ATM call, you're hoping your stock will get called away by month's end. The goal is to benefit from the generous option premium offered with an

ATM call while expecting exercise of your stock. Should this scenario pan out, you not only exit your stock position, but you could also generate some significant option income for the month, even with 100 shares.

Let's assume Willie Wonka is currently trading at $55. You would pop into your online brokerage account and check out the next month's option chain with a strike price closest to the current price. The option premium of an ATM call will be the highest for the strike price closest to the current stock price.

When looking at option chains, if the current month has less than one week left in the cycle, option premiums will tend to be on a significant decline. As expiration Friday approaches the decline accelerates even faster with ATM option premiums being worth just a few pennies on the last day. With just a week left, opt for the next month's option chain, which will have richer initial option premiums.

Shoot for an option return between 2 to 4 percent, your sweet spot for ATM calls. An option return of 3 percent for a 55 strike on 1 covered call should generate about $165 gross. This option strategy makes sense even when option fees convert back to the higher pre-2020 levels, since your stock has appreciated significantly in value and the actual cash amount of the option play also reflects this. In contrast, a much lower stock price results in a lower cash payout for your ATM option premium, which is impacted more by higher option fees. Something to keep in mind.

Some words of caution. Don't use this strategy if you suspect your stock to decline significantly in price over a short period of time. Both a fundamental and technical analysis of the current state of affairs should help you assess this probability. In all likelihood, this would mean having to buy back your call option at a higher cost than what you were initially paid, decreasing your overall returns. If you feel you've captured all the stock has to offer, just exit your position rather than chance a rapid decline in the stock's price.

Using an ATM call becomes an effective exit strategy, when your stock growth stalls and you're ready to exit your holding in anticipation of getting into another profitable momentum play.

Time to look at those two rolling strategies previously discussed in greater detail. These two strategies involve rolling one option contract from one month over to the next month. In doing so, you benefit from the monthly income stream being generated in the options market while the stock growth is either slowing or stalled.

Avoid using these strategies when the natural stock

appreciation momentum is greater than 3 percent per month. Mr. Market will reward you by just sitting on the stock. You'll expose yourself to less risk than if you were to layer on an options play.

However, should stock price appreciation be less than 3 percent per month, consider using a rolling strategy. For both of these case studies we're going to assume:

- You've purchased just 100 shares of stock.
- You've paid little or no transaction fees.
- You already have a covered call option in play on the stock.
- Expiration Friday is fast approaching.
- Your option contract is at or above the strike price for your contract.
- You would like to hold onto your stock.
- You would like to capture another monthly option premium.

Here's how you could capture future option premiums without being exercised.

Case Study #4: Generating Monthly Income with OTM Calls

When stock price appreciation slowly continues its upward climb, you can bolster your portfolio growth by selling next month's out-of-the-money call. In a slow growth situation, you're able to capture both the stock price appreciation along with a covered call premium for the month. This strategy works well under the following conditions:

- Overall market tone is positive.
- Stock's fundamentals continue to be rock solid.
- Mr. Market is still in favour with the stock.
- Stock price shows signs of continuing its upward price movement.

The strategy you'll be using involves closing your current month's option contract by buying back the original contract. In effect, you'll be buying back the equity you've benefitted from by seeing the stock appreciate in price. Once you've closed your current covered call, you're free to sell the next month's OTM strike price that's above the current stock price.

Your goal is to generate a small monthly income stream from writing covered calls while benefitting from a slowly rising stock price. Here's an example of how this scenario might pan out.

Let's assume you control 100 shares of Superman Cape Company (Cape), which you purchased last year for $20. In late June, you wrote a July (35) call when the stock was trading at $34 and you received an option premium of 50 cents per share. It's now the last week of July and the stock has already risen to $36.

You decide to buy back the equity in the stock by closing your option position with a buy-to-close order. You log into your brokerage account and place a limit order close to the ask price for the contract. To close your July option contract, you end up spending $2 per share.

Now, you're free to sell an August call option. In this case, you're going to select an out-of-the-money strike price of $37.50, which happens to be the closest OTM call to the current price of the stock. In doing so, you're able to obtain a monthly call premium of 40 cents per share, which is immediately deposited into your brokerage account.

Let's see what has transpired. You have used a combination of buying and selling option contracts to capture the price appreciation in the stock price and set yourself up for some additional upside potential. This has actually cost you some money to close and open these positions. Your total premium generated for July and August is a slight loss of $1.10 per share. This amount would have been paid out of your brokerage account to buy back the value in the stock.

Now, the value of your holding of Superman Cape Company has risen from $34 in late June to $36 in July.

This represents a 2.6 percent net increase after factoring in the cost of buying back the equity. The maximum upside potential for this combination of closing and opening transactions should Superman Cape close above the August (37.5) strike is 7 percent for a 2-month period of time.

By rolling forward and up, you can position yourself to take advantage of the price appreciation potential of the stock. This strategy works well when you would like to hang onto a stock that is starting to stall in momentum. Growth can be captured with out-of-the-money calls.

The last scenario we'll delve into is when you would like to generate a stream of income when your stock's momentum has stalled.

Case Study #5: Generating Income with ATM Calls

When stock price appreciation has stalled, you can capture at least another month of option premium, by selling an at-the-money call in this no growth environment. This strategy works well under the following conditions:

- Overall market tone is mixed.
- Stock's fundamentals continue to be solid but are slipping.

- Mr. Market no longer looks at the stock as being a market leader.
- Stock price movement shows signs of stalling.

As above, this strategy involves closing your current month's option contract by buying back the original contract, in essence buying back the equity. Once you close your current covered call, you'll sell the next month's ATM strike price closest to the current stock price.

Let's assume you sold one option contract of Hogwarts Butter Beer Company (BEER) stock with an October (25) strike for 40 cents when the current stock price was $24. Over the course of the month of October BEER rose from $24 per share to $25.10. Your October (25) option contract can be exercised at any time now. Based on your analysis of the state of affairs of the worldwide butter beer market and the Hogwarts Butter Beer Company in particular, you decide to use a rolling strategy to capture one last month of option income before exiting this stock holding.

To do so, you would need to buy back your October (25) option and sell a November (25) option right after. Selling the same strike price as the previous month takes advantage of the maximum option premiums available for the stock.

You discover that closing your October position will cost you approximately $1.15 to buy back the equity from an initial $24 to the current stock price of $25.10. Your next step is to sell a November (25) call, which nets you $1 per share.

Let's examine what has transpired. You initially earned 40 cents per share for selling your OTM call. Closing this position cost you $1.15 per share. And selling the next month's same strike gave you $1 per share. Your option premium profits netted you 25 cents per share. You've also bought up the value of your stock to the (25) strike.

With BEER trading above the (25) strike, you can expect to be called away at any time. Should this happen you would benefit from over 5 percent of equity and option income growth over the 2-month period of time. If BEER had been trading sideways over this same period of time, you would have still generated a significant gain by implementing this rolling forward strategy.

As you can see from walking through the five case studies, it's possible to augment your returns by selectively using just a handful of covered call option strategies. These conservative strategies can be quite effective when you've adopted a momentum trading approach.

Hopefully, these case studies have helped you better understand the income producing potential offered by using covered calls with your momentum plays. Now, it's time to delve deeper into how you could become a more effective investor in the final upcoming chapter.

CREATING AN EFFECTIVE INVESTMENT PLAN

THE FOCUS of this final chapter is to put the entire momentum trading approach into the broader perspective of consistently generating returns from your stock investments. The underlying premise is that you control how you invest. Mr. Market controls how and when you'll get paid.

Before delving into what an effective investment plan might look like, it may be helpful to explore how you can increase the probability of coming out on top with each of your positions. In other words, what would it take to develop a winning edge in the stock market?

Developing Your Winning Edge:

The one sage piece of advice most experienced or professional investors would give is to "learn before you earn". You've taken the first step to doing so, by picking up this resource and using it to fuel your insatiable desire to generate consistent returns in the stock market.

This is only the beginning. Continue to push your comfort zone by exploring other means by which you can augment your wealth. Whether you're motivated to reduce the effects of financial hardship, replace income from a lost job, rebuild your retirement funds or just provide a better life for your family, it's through education you'll be able to accomplish these objectives.

I've always believed that when you stop learning, you stop living. Quenching your thirst for knowledge starts by setting aside time devoted to improving your financial intelligence. For many this means blocking out quiet time during the day. And mornings tend to work well for many. When you're fresh, your mind is ready to absorb what is thrown at it like a sponge wipes up a soup spill.

For some, the morning commute, gym workout or Fido's pee-pee break offer opportune times to improve your financial education. Many such individuals gravitate to listening to audiobooks because of the level of convenience in being able to multi-task.

.   .   .

Keeping It Simple:

Whatever approach you eventually take to investing, keep your investment system simple. The simpler the better. Believe it or not, there are more important priorities in life than being totally absorbed in managing and monitoring your particular investment system. Spending quality time with family and friends, improving your overall fitness level, ensuring you're healthy are values we all should hold dear to us.

Your investing should be a means to an end; a means by which you can achieve your desired lifestyle for you and your family. Simplification and automation of any investment approach frees up time for you to pursue the finer things in life.

When investing you will experience loss. It's a natural part of the experience. Often losses present a unique learning opportunity from which you can move your investing prowess to the next level. All famous investors and business tycoons have experienced loss. We all make mistakes. It's how we learn.

Take full responsibility for your actions when things don't work out as planned. Don't blame Mr. Market, your second cousin twice removed or your pet iguana. Work through those frustrations and challenges with the sole intent purpose of becoming a better more consistently successful investor.

As you undertake employing this momentum approach, focus your attention on limiting loss and reducing risk. Keep your positions small. Spread out your capital. Monitor your holdings on a regular basis. Determine your entry and exit point for every opportunity. And record these on paper. As a do-it-yourself investor, focus your efforts, letting one success fuel others.

Planning for Success:

When you're willing to risk your hard-earned capital in any investment opportunity always go with a well-formulated plan. Your plan should outline a step-by-step process by which you'll be able to guide the outcomes in a positive direction. When it comes to stock investing, there are four key elements you need to think through for your trading plan:

1. An entry mechanism that determines precisely what triggers a buy decision.
2. How you're going to deal with risk? What will you do if a position moves against you, or if the reason you bought the stock changes suddenly?
3. How are you going to lock in your profits?
4. How will you position size, and when will you decide to reallocate funds?

Hope is not a plan. This is why you need to follow specific rules or criteria that'll guide your decision-making. When determining those specific entry and exit criteria you're going to follow for a particular holding it may be helpful to frame them using if-then statements.

If-then statements are common in contingency planning and habit reversal training. Using these conditional statements provides you with an action plan to follow when a condition has been met. Here are some of the most important situations to consider developing "what if ... then" statements:

- When will you exit a position should it go against you?
- What must a stock be doing to be considered for purchase again in the event you get stopped out of the trade?
- What specific criteria will you follow for selling into strength and nailing down a decent gain?
- When do you sell into weakness to protect your profit?
- How will you handle catastrophic situations or sudden changes requiring swift action under pressure?

We've covered these and other investment decisions in this guide. However, to really internalize your decision-making matrix its helpful taking a moment to create and write down specific guidelines that'll govern your actions. Call them rules or conditional statements, they all serve the same purpose, allowing you greater control and accountability for your actions.

You've been exposed to a specific investment plan using a momentum investing approach along with occasional covered call option plays. You may choose to use it as is or modify the approach to best suit your current reality. At a minimum your plan must include these four factors:

1. An initial stop-loss level or exit strategy in place.
2. Re-entry criteria should you be forced to exit any position.
3. Criteria for selling at a profit.
4. A disaster plan for each position you enter.

The bottom line is that capital preservation should be top of mind at all times when investing. You need to constantly assess risk to capital loss and put into place plans that minimize any unlikely outcomes. Your priorities in order of importance are to:

- Limit your loss. Initiate exit strategies quickly.
- Protect your breakeven line. Monitor your breakeven point closely.
- Protect your profit. Use a trailing stop or back stop so sizeable gains don't slip away.

All of these measures require you to become actively engaged in the investment process. Avoid just buying, holding and praying your initial investment will go up. You want to avoid "dead money" investments. Non-performing positions cost you in potential returns and the lost opportunity by parking your money.

No need to spend hours at a time glued in front of your computer screen to be successful in the stock market. There are finer things in life to pursue than watching a ticker tape crawl across your screen. Being an actively engaged stock investor need not take up a lot of your time. Once you have your investment plan up and running, a few minutes each day should be all you'll need to monitor and maintain your income generation machine.

CONCLUSION

You began your journey into the wonderful world of stock investing by initially exploring how momentum investing fits into the overall stock investment picture. We looked at how value, income and growth investing influence momentum investing, providing the framework from which your guide is built upon.

You learned about the pros and cons of using such an approach. More importantly, you discovered which three types of businesses make good potential momentum investment plays, namely:

1. Emerging, fast-growing companies.
2. Formula companies capable of rapid expansion.

3. Rapid reversal companies who've been unfairly beaten up in the markets.

You also found out which types of companies to avoid. Certain businesses do not make good momentum plays because of various inherent conditions. Often mature, well established icons dishing out quarterly dividends don't offer the best momentum play opportunities.

In Chapter 2, we delved into what the business or economic cycle is all about and when to expect the economy to rebound. You specifically looked at what was being done to deal with the current crisis - the global COVID-19 pandemic.

To get a better feel as to how the pandemic is affecting the global economy, we addressed the impact of the coronavirus on each of the eleven economic sectors that make up the overall stock market. Along with these insights, you glimpsed into the world of the institutional investor and how sectors are affected by big market moves by these players.

Chapter 3 saw you diving deeper into identifying those industries impacted the most by the pandemic. You found out how the BEACH stocks were shaken up. More specifically, you discovered which specific industries have radically changed moving forward and those exceptions to the rule to observe and watch out for. This chapter also gave you insights into those industries the least affected by the recent downturn in events.

Having a better idea as to how certain industries have been impacted, Chapter 4 addressed how to find momentum stocks. You learned about what has changed in the stock selection process and how herd immunity affects the overall stock market.

More importantly, you found out how to narrow down your stock picks, which industries will be slower to recover, and those that'll bounce back faster. Finally, you picked up tips on where to look for these prospects.

Chapter 5 saw you analyzing your prospects. You discovered how to initially screen for momentum prospects and how to assess the profitability of each candidate. You began focusing your attention on just a handful of selection criteria, namely:

- Revenue growth rate.
- Return on Invested Capital.
- Earnings per Share Growth rate.
- Quarterly Analyst Earnings Estimates.

- 50-day and 200-day Simple Moving Averages.
- Stock Trading Volume.
- Relative Strength Index.
- Moving Average Divergence Convergence.

Along with these eight indicators, you found out which buy signals to look for and what is the best approach to purchasing your stocks. You also picked up a number of insights into when to best time your entry into the market.

In Chapter 6 you explored when you should exit your stock positions. The chapter was all about managing risk and locking in profits. You picked up a few simple exit signals to abide by. We also emphasized limiting risk with small positions, limiting transaction fees in the future and reducing your overall risk by selling call options.

Chapter 7 had you enter the world of options trading. We specifically explored why you should occasionally use monthly covered calls on stock you own. Options provides you with three key benefits:

1. Options create monthly income.
2. They reduce portfolio risk.
3. Options accelerate wealth creation.

You also found out how easy it is to enter the options market. When selling an option contract, you needed to enter four bits of information:

- The expiration date for the contract.
- The strike price for the option.
- The number of option contracts.
- The desired premium price.

In Chapter 8, you discovered how to best enter the options market. We started by ensuring you're working with the right broker. You also found out what five key selection criteria to use to increase your option trading success. And finally, you picked up what type of order to place when selling covered calls.

Chapter 9 was all about option strategies. Here, we focused on just two strategies you'll end up using the vast majority of the time with a momentum investing approach. You learned about the growth generation strategy and how to put it into play. You also learned how to use an income generation strategy and when it's most opportune to do so. In this case, rich option premiums can be used to augment overall returns when your momentum play stalls.

In Chapter 10, you were introduced to how to safely exit your option positions. This involved finding out when it's appropriate to use an exit strategy. You picked up two key strategies - rolling forward and up and rolling forward. Each of these strategies are designed to generate additional portfolio growth by carrying one open position forward into the next month.

Chapter 11 was all about putting much of the theory into practice. We walked through two momentum stock case studies with both small and large positions. Then, we looked at using a covered call to exit a momentum play. Finally, you learned how to generate income with out-of-the-money and at-the-money monthly call options.

Your final chapter capped everything off by glimpsing at how to develop your winning edge in the stock market. Much of the emphasis was placed on keeping your investment approach as simple as possible. Along with this was the notion of developing and following an investment plan. Planning for success is a key factor in the overall momentum investment approach.

This investment guide focused on sharing an investment approach well-suited for recovering from the current economic downturn. However, the basic principles discussed can be applied to other major stock market corrections. Use the same approach to find, analyze, strategize and time your momentum plays. The context may change but the overall approach remains the same.

If you enjoyed this book or if you found that you've gained greater insights into how you could conceivably build a better lifestyle, then I'd be very grateful if you'd post a positive review on Amazon.

Your support does matter and it really does make a difference. The feedback and encouragement will help me continue to write the kind of books that help you get results.

If you'd like to leave a review, then all you need to do is go to the customer review section on the book's Amazon page. You'll then see a big button that says: "Write a customer review" - click that and you're good to go.

Thanks again for your support.

In closing, should you like some additional advice into stock investing, I encourage you to pick up a copy of the special report "Momentum Investing Rules". You'll receive some great insights along with an extensive list of rules addressed in your book.

MOMENTUM INVESTING RULES

SPECIAL REPORT

(You may struggle making serious money without knowing these ...)

This special report covers:

- Why the "right rules" increase your probability of success.

- How to increase your confidence by being "in the zone".
- What 7 types of rules you need to follow - no matter the approach.
- More than 3 dozen specific rules to protect your capital and generate income.

To receive your special report and discover how to invest in momentum stocks with greater confidence, check out the link below:

https://successorizeyourself.activehosted.com/f/5

Enjoy the additional insights and updates.

Scott

TO YOUR ONGOING SUCCESS AS AN
INVESTOR!